Lonely Heart, Will Travel

Richard La Plante

Escargot Books and Music

Lonely Heart, Will Travel

LONELY HEART, WILL TRAVEL

Many of my characters in *Lonely Heart, Will Travel* are based upon composites of women I dated during the course of my online experiences. All incidences are true, some out of context, others as they occurred. Physical descriptions have been altered as have certain geographical locations. It is not my intent to injure feelings or expose others to criticism or self-doubt. I give thanks for every lesson learned.

ISBN 978-1-908191-40-3 Paperback

Cover Design: Michele Hauf

Escargot Books and Music
Ojai, California

for Elizabeth

Acknowledgements

Mayo, my stalwart ally, always. Arthur, Jill, and Ingrid, who got me through some pretty tough times — thank you. Sandy for her deep intuition and magical cards. Julie for watery coffee and sheer energy. Jimmy B, my one-man sounding board and honest critic. My Zoom Reading Group, who allow me to reflect and read — you mean the world to me. Mark, for his spiritual friendship and glasses of wine. My sons, Jack and Tomas, for never letting me take any of this too seriously. My Zoom Breathing Group — inhale, exhale, pause and relax. I love you. And special thanks to the late Penny, the chihuahua, for her unconditional love.

~1~

I'd left the light on in an adjoining bathroom and the bed was cast in a dim borrowed glow, a milky white. We were making love when I sensed something, a feeling of loneliness that swept over me like a devil's kiss. I opened my eyes. Looking down at her. Beautiful; she'd always been beautiful to me, her dark hair fanning out against the sheets, long regal face, full lips and deep brown eyes. Eyes that were open, like mine. Looking up. Eyes that I had known for fifteen years, from London to New York, from the sandy dunes of Long Island to this small, high desert town in Southern California. Lover's eyes. Mother's eyes. Eyes that had seen the birth of two sons, my wonderful sons, her wonderful sons, sons sleeping now in twin beds in a room down the hallway. Eyes that had seen me laugh and cry and rage. Eyes that knew everything about me, the strong and the weak, the rough and the raw. I loved those eyes. I trusted them. But now they were different; there was deadness inside them, something vacant and far away. Something I had never seen before. Unnerving as I felt her body stiffen and lose its warmth. Her mouth was set, like a shadowed line across her face, but it was her eyes that spoke. I tried to block what they told me but that was impossible. Besides, I needed to know. So, I listened. I could not help but listen, as if their message was ordained. Loneliness returned. Gone, the eyes said, I'm gone from you, and I can never return. Simple as that, final and forever. The sensation began in my gut and traveled upwards, seeking my heart like a dagger. In that dim light I was open, vulnerable. With our sleeping children down the hall. In that terrible vacuum of silence, the dagger entered.

"Why?" I asked, arching up and pulling back, shrinking inside her.

She stared. Said nothing. Just stared, as if she'd entered some kind of shock, some dreadful irrevocable realization of her own.

"What's wrong?" My voice edgy this time.

She never blinked. Shook her head slowly. A tear? Were there tears in her eyes?

No words as she turned her head away, pulling back against the pillow. Separating our bodies. Leaving nothing but cold space.

"Say something," I urged.

She looked at me, frightened, as if in an instant I had become an intruder, someone strange and unwelcome. Demanding a currency she didn't possess.

"Talk to me. Tell me what is wrong."

Still nothing.

"Are you okay?" I asked.

Raising my voice. "Damn it. Say something."

Her face seemed to solidify with resolution, as if whatever she had felt or seen was now born true. She pulled the sheet to her body, covering her naked breasts.

"Why are you doing this?" I demanded.

She shook her head as I jerked away, standing up. Hovering above her.

"Why?"

Silence.

Then, "I'm out of here."

Marching from the bedroom, furious and self-righteous. Up the stairs to the guest room. Under the covers. Staring at the ceiling. Alone.

The next day, her ring finger was bare. The diamond from Argentina set in a flat gold band was gone. The marriage was over.

Looking back, I wish I had controlled my anger, been more sensitive, calmer, more the lover, less the fighter; but in many ways I was a different person then. Still, I recognize the man in that memory, and I forgive him his anger, his indignation, his arrogance, I forgive him all the things that were the catalyst for his change. A change that took lots of time and lots of pain.

***

~2~

We are locked together because of our two sons, and a "dream" house that we began several years before that dark night in the bedroom. A dream that has consumed most of our savings and all of our time.

Officially separated, friendly but no longer intimate. We talk, generally about our sons or the nightmare building project we've undertaken. Now it's my oldest son's thirteenth birthday and we're in Big Bear, a ski resort about 80 miles northeast of Los Angeles; the birthday boy wants to see some snow. We have one giant room, with a hot plate and a minifridge. Sleeping arrangements include the boys on twin cots and mom and dad in the California King with a long body pillow lying lengthwise between them. This is a non-contact event, not even the stray foot.

Snow is falling.

We rent four sonic snow saucers, plastic discs with side handles, and take to the hills, sliding and gliding, until we are the only ones there, surrounded by trees turning white as the sun sets and the laughter fades, like an echo in time, and there's that hollow feeling again. Taking me over. This is it. My family. All I've got, and its splintering.

We drive home, back to school for the boys, back to the building project for the estranged mom and dad. The new house includes 21 acres of raw land, the majority of it unusable, all hills and gullies, and the side of a mountain. After countless delays imposed upon us by the county and their overly stringent building inspector, the house is still a frame, waiting on top of the hill like a ravenous jackal.

We continue in silence. There's no palpable hostility, just the fact that we don't have much to say to each other. My wife was never a big talker anyway, tending to clam-up when angry or upset, which may explain why I was taken by surprise when the marriage ended. She never said she was unhappy, and I never saw the break-up coming. When I asked her why, she answered, "I don't know." Until I grew to hate those three words. "I don't know." We have discussed all of this in the presence of several marriage counselors, and the most she offered was that she felt numb, going through the motions of life, suffocated by me and the small town that I chose as our home. Explaining that she will be my partner in the building of the house and in raising the boys but as far as the marriage goes, it's over. I'm hurt, frightened, and the dissolution of my family saddens me beyond anything I've known. A solo dad, single at 64. Alone. Or "on the loose," as a seventy-one-year-old movie star friend described it. Like I'm going to be the apple of many eyes. The king of the retirement village. Somehow it doesn't feel that way. Not at this point, anyway.

Onwards, up the winding driveway that takes us on a near vertical path to the money-pit. There it sits, a long wooden frame, the skeleton of my tomorrows. We are meeting the representative from the company that will manufacture our custom doors and windows; naturally, everything has to be custom, because our eccentric Argentinian architect, last spotted several months ago boarding a flight to Uruguay, designed the house with no regard for costs or anything else resembling standard construction. Leaving it to us to figure out how to pay for it.

Months pass, a year, with many financial struggles and many delays imposed by the county building inspector, but finally the house is ready. The family moves in, mom and dad no longer separated by a long body pillow but legally separated by a long, polished concrete corridor that ends in two separate bedrooms. Marriage counselors have been replaced by lawyers. She keeps going to London and I've given up caring what's at the other end of her plane ride; I'm a free man, or at least I tell myself that I am. Several friends confirm this new freedom by setting me up with various women in various locations. I fall in love instantly, and always before I've met any of my new mail order brides. In this case, it's email order since that's how the interaction inevitably begins, with an exchange of pleasantries, leading to a little flirting, leading to an exchange of photographs which are generally very glamourous and ten years out of date, including my own, leading to a phone call, leading to long car drives to far-away places. Leading to, "Oh my God, that can't be the same person as the one in the photograph." Possibly on both ends. Leading to a fast retreat. But I'm willing to do it; in fact, I'm excited to because I know that new love is right around the corner, if I just keep driving.

Then I am introduced to Ann. She's from Los Angeles, has the most incredible green eyes, sense of style and slight English accent, a leftover from her London roots. She's also seventy-five years old, has severe scoliosis and generally travels by walker. Ann and I hit it off instantly. One meeting at lunch and I know all about her upbringing, from hustling on the streets of Soho before graduating to full Hollywood madam, procuring all manner of sex and contraband for the rich and famous. She's worked in varying capacities on movie sets and in record studios and has been close friends with everyone from Marlon Brando to Jim Morrison. She's a little lady who has lived an extra-large life. Now, she's pretty much confined to a rent controlled one-bedroom apartment with three dogs, a couple of cats, a parrot that resides on her shoulder and a squeaky walker. I love characters, and I love Ann. The feeling seems mutual as she promises to pull out all the stops and find me just the right woman. I imagine her breaking out an old Rolodex and leafing through her vintage list of favorites, which is exactly what she does. A week later my cell phone rings.

"How is my favorite darling today?"

"Ann?"

"You're going to love Michelle," she continues.

"Michelle?"

"Absolutely. She was with Jack for a while and I believe she spent some time with Mick on Mustique before being engaged to Warren. She's fabulously gorgeous and she's perfect for you."

I don't even ask who these names belong to, but I assume they are big-name actors, of a certain era, with maybe one major rock star thrown in, a bit intimidating.

"Yeah, but Ann, why would Michelle be interested in me?"

"Because, darling, you are an absolutely fabulous man, and I've told her all about you and she is very, very interested."

Now, you've got to understand that self-confidence and self-esteem can run at all-time lows in the midst of separation and probable divorce, particularly with the long-time absence of any intimate physical contact; I've driven down the main drag of town, eyeing couples from the window of my car and wondered how they do it. Figuring that whatever the guy has going for him, no matter how short, tall, thin, obese, rich, poor or unattractive he is, that he has something that I apparently lack, since I have been irrevocably rejected. Destined to drive the streets alone, glued to the lyrics of old heartbreak songs, like "You've Lost that Loving Feeling" on the radio while gazing at the happy people walking by. So, the idea that someone, anyone, is interested in me makes me very, very excited, providing that beautiful sensation of hope, like a light at the end of a black tunnel, albeit a small flame from a single candle.

"Thank you, Ann," I say, feeling and sounding humble.

"I'm going to put you in touch," she adds. "Take down this number. She's expecting you to call her."

I'm seated in my office, which is a small room with a chair, a desk and a computer, built next to the garage and away from the main house, so I have a sense of privacy as I write the number down on a yellow legal pad, the same pad I use to work out what I'll be worth after a division of assets, then double check it by reading the phone number back to her, twice.

Ann obviously doesn't mess around. "Call her right now, she's expecting to hear from you," she insists. "Then call me back. I want to know how it goes. Good luck, darling."

Click …

I'm on the spot. Nervous. What if I blow it, with a quaking voice and nothing clever to say, or what if my self-diagnosed Tourette syndrome kicks in and I blurt out something inappropriate or obscene? I mean, this lady, Michelle, has reputedly traveled in high circles, and I'm not exactly at the top of my game, living on dwindling book royalties, pacing the floors at night, avoiding my own reflection in the mirror while confined to the solo barracks of my "dream" house. Hardly an A-lister. Still, if I want Ann's respect, and her continuing help in finding me a partner, or at least a date, I'd better make the call. I look through the glass door of my phone booth-sized office. I can see the front of the main house. There's no movement. Somehow, I feel like I'm cheating on my wife, even though I haven't shared a bed with her in almost three years and yesterday she informed me that she's going to London for a month to begin renovations on a family-owned apartment. Yeah, right, I'm nearly certain there's a man involved in those renovations, but I can't prove it and, at this point, it's none of my business. I pick up the phone and try to enter a Zen no-negative-thought state as I dial the number.

"Hello …" the voice on the other end is slightly gravelly, like a whisky voice, or maybe a smoker's voice, a voice that's walked the red carpet, slept with stars, and is now talking to me.

"Hello, this is …"

'Richard," she says. "Ann said you'd call."

"Yes, and here I am." And that's the extent of my fast repartee.

Michelle takes it from there and pretty soon we exchange email addresses and agree to send each other pictures. I get off the phone, once again feeling that great and fleeting sensation of hope; maybe being single is not such a bad thing; in fact, it's exciting. In fact, I am really glad I'm free as I hunt down a not so recent black and white portrait, taken by my in name only wife who just happens to be a very good photographer. The photo is flattering, giving me a sort of movie star flair, with a good hairline and wide, confident smile. Off it goes with a whoosh and a prayer. Within minutes I receive a return email from Michelle. Now things are really heating up. I open it and voilà, there she is, full bosomed, very full, in a swimsuit and poised on the cusp of a gently rolling surf, all white teeth and legs. Like something from the *Sports Illustrated* swimsuit edition. Being single just got infinitely more attractive. Like, maybe it's the best thing that has ever happened to me. Meant to be. I email back and say the photo has arrived and tell her she's beautiful. She emails me again and says she likes my picture and suggests we meet in person. Closing with, "We're going to have some fun." In my state of deprivation, I interpret this as a potential sexual invitation, which both excites and terrifies me, since I sure don't want to come off badly if compared with the likes of the famous womanizers Michelle has reportedly been involved with. Particularly if she reports any inadequacy or lack of performance to Madam Ann, who is not known for her discretion and is known to spend hours gossiping on a telephone that seems to have attached itself to her ear, interrupted only by her parrot yelling a succession of *fuck you*'s and *kiss my ass* from his perch on her shoulder. A poor performance could end my future chances for romance in one call.

I contemplate visiting my local GP to acquire a prescription for Viagra, then doubling the dose before the imagined event. But my GP is a woman and I'm too proud to discuss ED. Besides, I don't even know if I have ED, it's been so long. I assume it still works. I mean, why wouldn't it? Atrophied, but functional.

Besides, I've only tried the little blue pill once before, without my partner's knowledge, and that was a catastrophe, resulting in a vicious headache, sweating palms and my wife, when she still was "my wife," falling sound asleep beside me, snoring gently as I admired the effects of the pill and contemplated her displeasure if I woke her up. It was a long, restless night.

And the words, "have some fun" do not necessarily mean nonstop sex, or even a soft kiss for that matter. I'm just desperate, lonely, slightly confused, and very excited that Michelle actually wants to meet me. I dismiss the Viagra and make the bold decision to travel "au natural."

So far, so good. Things are moving. She invites me to Pasadena, which is where she lives. I accept instantly, suddenly full of energy, more energy than I've had in years, feeling that I've just discovered the new love of my life. I can now officially stop envying couples on the sidewalk. *Lonely days are gone. I'm a goin' home. My baby just wrote me a letter.* Pulsing with excitement is the only way I can describe it.

I'm soon booked into a suite at The Langham in Pasadena, featuring a four-poster bed, which looks stately, and at two hundred and fifty dollars a night on Expedia is the most up-market place I can find. I am not a poser and I am not wealthy, but I am slightly intimidated by Ann's description of Michelle, not to mention the swimsuit photograph, and I don't want to be spotted coming out of a Motel 6, not for a first impression. Plus, since my wife is going to London next Tuesday and I will be alone with the boys for several weeks, driving to and from school and preparing one-star dinners that are less than well-received, I need to fast-track this potential relationship.

Then I call Madam Ann. She's a step ahead of me, having already spoken to Michelle.

"She loves you, darling. Says you sound absolutely fun and absolutely fabulous. And she thinks you're absolutely handsome." Which, I may have been, ten years ago, when the photograph was taken.

Following Michelle's endorsement and still traveling on a chariot of hot air, I announce my Saturday departure to my imminent ex, who at this point, asks no questions other than my date of return.

"Sometime Sunday, maybe late."

Then, I count the days till the fated rendezvous, trying to keep my imagination in check. The truth is, I have not been alone in a bedroom with a woman in about two years. Sex is a vague and distant memory. Still, I'm thinking about it; in fact, I can't stop thinking about it, especially when re-visiting the swimsuit email, which I do at hourly intervals. I go over my wardrobe several times, laying out several shirts acquired in my London heydays, a few un-wine-stained T-shirts, socks, underwear, shoes. It looks like I'm planning a European vacation, something that might last a month or two, when in fact I'm giving myself options, lots of options.

I feel like a man adrift at sea. Praying for rescue.

Ahoy, Michelle!

*

~3~

The Langham embraces me in all its four-poster splendor as I unpack my clothes, shower, shave for the second time in a day and change into fresh jeans and a gray Iron & Resin T-shirt, which comes from a shop in Ventura that features a black '57 panhead Harley in the window, just kind of place, at least it was thirty year ago. Then, I sit down on the side of the bed, take a few calming breaths and dial Michelle's number. Is it better to begin with a more formal "Hello, it's Richard," or a more confident and casual "Hi, Michelle, it's me"? Her cell phone rings many times, giving me plenty of opportunity to contemplate the "hi" or "hello" dilemma, until: "Hi, this is Michelle, I'm not here right now but if you leave me a message, maybe I'll return your call."

Paranoia descends like a wet leather jacket.

Maybe. Did she just say *maybe*? This is dire, or it could be. She knew I was coming. I even emailed her the approximate time of my arrival. Maybe?

I leave a message.

"Hello, Michelle, it's Richard. I'm here at The Langham." Leave my cell number and wait.

Alone in The Langham, lying on the hard mattress of the reproduction 15th century bed, all dressed up with nowhere to go, my recent life washes over me like a wave of dirty dish water. There's no way back to my marriage, especially now that we are lawyered up and trying to resolve our situation with family law, which means no ugly court hearings and fights over money and custody; all the stuff that ruins lives, particularly the lives of the children who must watch from the sidelines. So far, an air of civility has reigned during the group meetings which take place in the

Oxnard office of my wife's lawyer, who I occasionally mistake as an ally until he gets up and jots financial figures down on his standing chalkboard. The entire process carries a weight of sadness, particularly when he says solemnly, "You're going to need to sell the house." Then there's my writing career, which has stalled with a lack of product and no real interest in writing, as my royalties become hundreds, not thousands of dollars a month. Nothing like a bout of depression to dull the creative process. Until the process stops altogether and finding love, any kind of love, becomes the overriding impetus to get out of bed in the morning. Plus, there's this strange stiffness in my shoulders, which I attribute to swimming laps in the local pool; although I've been swimming for years and never felt anything like this before.

All in all, I'm not in a good way and the longer I stare at the white ceiling while running disaster movies through my mental projector, the worse and more foolish I feel. What the fuck am I doing at The Langham, an old guy in young clothes?

My cell phone rings.

It's Michelle, full-throated and sexy, as if she's done this a thousand times; maybe she has. "Sorry baby, I was in the bath, getting ready."

My negative self-image fades with the distant thunder of twin exhaust pipes.

"What room are you in?" she asks.

I'm back in the saddle, all custom chrome and leathers.

"415," I answer.

"See you there in about half an hour."

"Great. I'm really looking forward to it, Michelle."

I put down the phone. Half an hour. That's just about enough to brush my teeth a few times, finger-comb my hair into several flattering positions, stand in the mirror and check my pecs beneath the soft cotton of the Iron & Resin T-shirt, smile broadly at myself from varying angles, wondering how I compare to the decade old photograph she's seen, adjust the lights in the room to allow for the decade and invade the minifridge to procure a mini bottle of extremely overpriced Johnny Walker Red, hoping it will smooth some of the rougher edges of my face.

Half an hour passes, still no Michelle. Another finger-comb, a glance towards the minifridge. Tempted by Johnny Walker. My cell rings. Michelle's voice fills the airways.

"Hi baby, I'm just around the corner. Room 415, right?"

A quick check of my entrance key and I answer. "Yes, 415."

"On my way."

A last-minute light check, using the dimmers to create flattering reflections of myself in the mirror, a quick mouth rinse so I don't smell like an alcoholic and there's a quiet knock on the door. One slow breath to calm my nerves and I answer.

"Hi."

"Hi," I reply.

Michelle is taller than I am, which makes her above five-nine, and she's very blonde with full collagen lips and breasts that I can only describe as pneumatic, bursting forward from a pink sequined T-shirt. She's wearing tight faded jeans and strapped sandals with slight heels. She smiles. It's a super-sized smile, in keeping with everything else about her.

"Well, Richard, are we just gonna' stand here or are you going to invite me in?"

I step aside, grateful that, at least, she recognizes me from the photograph.

"Please … Come in."

She brushes past with a sultry hint of musk and sits down in one of the twin leather chairs that flank a wooden coffee table at the foot of the four-poster.

I feel very at ease with Michelle as I sit on the edge of the bed facing her. She seems totally relaxed which has a calming effect on me.

"Would you like a drink?"

"Sure."

I get up, walk to the corner and open the minifridge, calling out a list of available beverages.

Johnny Walker makes another appearance and we split a mini bottle, then spend the next fifteen minutes talking about Ann, who Michelle has known for nearly thirty years, and the strange assortment of wildlife that inhabits her tiny apartment, particularly the foul-mouthed parrot who rarely leaves her shoulder. We laugh and it occurs to me that I haven't had a good laugh with a woman in a very long time.

"Where would you like to eat?" I ask.

Michelle suggests a local Italian restaurant and off we go. A glass of red Barbera later and I feel like I'm on a Roman holiday with one of my greatest friends. We exit the restaurant hand in hand and drive the few miles to The Langham extremely carefully. Nothing like a DUI to ruin a new romance. Then comes the awkward, "Would you like a cup of coffee?" moment. I am about to suggest walking Michelle to her car when she asks, "Do you have any red wine in your little fridge?"

"Absolutely," I answer although I don't recall seeing any. I just want the evening to continue and in my current state of intoxication, which is probably above the legal limit to drive a car and definitely enough to give me a warm, relaxed feeling of confidence that I haven't experienced in years, I wrap my arm around her shoulder as we walk the quiet, gray-carpeted corridor to 415. Inside and to the fridge. A small bottle of Cabernet waits patiently. I rinse the whiskey glasses and pour.

"I don't want to go crazy," Michelle says, sipping the wine. "Or I'll have to spend the night here."

"Please go crazy," I suggest.

We end up lying on the bed, kissing passionately as I am reassured that a visit to the doctor's office was not necessary. Michelle is marvelous; she has a way of making me feel good about myself. After half an hour of oral exploration she stands up and begins to remove her clothing, starting with her pink sequined T-shirt, revealing a drowning man's fantasy, two flotation devices of gigantic proportion. They may not exactly be real, but she carries them with such authority that reality no longer matters; the faded jeans soon join the sparkling sequins on the floor as she looks down at me.

"I warned you."

I move over and invite her to lie down. She does. We kiss a little more and that's it. She's drowsy, and I am suddenly not so interested in sex, more in having a woman lying next to me, and somehow I believe that Michelle feels the same way. It's like a creature comfort, two warm bodies, sheltered from the storm. My storm is the break-up of my family; I'm not certain of hers, not then, anyway, but I do realize that beyond all the hype of who we want to be and what we would like to be perceived as being, there is the heart, and as Carson McCullers said in the title of her 1940s novel, *The Heart Is a Lonely Hunter.*

Things don't end in Pasadena. Michelle is fun, real and high-voltage, up for anything as our adventures extend to an evening in the hot springs of Palm Desert which features naked bathing in the outdoor springs followed by her presenting me with a crotchless, black and white striped jump suit, donned after several glasses of wine.

God it feels good to be young again.

Our romance lasts several months as it winds its way to Carpinteria, and a hotel with a sea view. These one-night excursions with Michelle have become a wellness tonic for my frequent states of melancholia, which include fears for my future and guilt that I could have prevented the past. It's tough for me to simply let go and move on. Until a new reality strikes after a raucous evening of tequila, public kissing at the dinner table and loud guitar playing on the seaside veranda; yes, I brought my guitar, while the other guests, all trying to have a quiet evening, cast scowling glances. We are the couple that others avoid, or report to the concierge with a request for immediate eviction. Following the dinner serenade, we have a noisy night in the bedroom. All going fine till the dawn's early light. I'm showered, shaved and dressed. Ready to head down to LA for a business meeting, trying to sell an Amazon company an original idea for home audio entertainment, and not really considering when the next rendezvous with Michelle will occur. I just take it for granted that she enjoys these brief encounters as much as I do, with no strings attached.

She is seated on the edge of the bed, watching me prepare to leave. "You know, I was a great wife," she says. Her words contain a certain gravity, and catch me unprepared. I lay the bag down on the floor and turn towards her.

"Yes ... I'll bet you were," I reply.

Michelle's heartache is that she is widowed, having been married to a prominent film producer. In love with her late husband, she watched him battle cancer and die, still in his forties. She has been by herself for ten years and, sometimes, I feel the sadness all around her.

"I'd like to be married again, someday," she says.

I feel a bit of a jerk. Assuming that these brief encounters were all that either of us wanted, or needed, when in fact, I get to return to a house with two young sons and a wife, albeit an estranged wife who lives in a room down the hall, but at least she's there, and in many ways, I'm still attached. While Michelle goes home to an empty apartment.

"Someone special, who'll be with me forever," she whispers.

Suddenly Michelle looks younger, innocent, her face more like the smiling picture she sent me before life etched its stories into her skin.

I hesitate before answering, "You know I'm not ready for that."

Silence.

Then, smiling, trying to lighten things up. "But until that person comes along, maybe I can fill in."

She looks at me with a mixture of anger and sadness, or maybe it's pity as I bend down and kiss her on the forehead, grab my bag and leave. Down the 101 South. Pondering our last interaction and regretting my final, insensitive words. In LA, stuck at a traffic light on Wilshire Boulevard when my phone pings. I look down at it.

"Please never call, email or text me again ... Michelle."

*

Living in a divided house and fearing the breakup of my family creates desperation. No amount of intellectual acrobatics, like telling myself that over half of marriages end in divorce, that the kids will survive unscathed or that I will meet someone else and live happily ever after, serves to quell my fears and anxieties. Sleeping becomes impossible as my imagination takes me to negative places, usually involving a tottering and broken old man living his last days with the sensation of a wasted, pointless, loveless life. My greatest therapy is a nightly telephone call to my best friend, who lives about two hours away, a man I have known for thirty years, from London to Los Angeles; he is a veteran of three divorces, two to the same woman. He listens; he understands.

"It gets better," he reassures me. "It all heals with time. But first, you've got to let go. It's over. Let it go."

Then, one evening, at ten o'clock, I place the customary call for consolation and get a message machine. He is good about returning calls, and regular, and usually gets back to me within minutes, but this night is different. He doesn't answer. Nor does he return my calls the following morning, or the next evening. By the third night, I am very worried and phone his ex-wife; she is equally concerned, since they are in regular contact and he has not returned her calls either.

Later the following afternoon, a mutual friend finds my best friend face down on his kitchen floor. Dead for three days, a heart attack.

I'm suffering... He's dead.

Ultimately, life is all about letting go. And I'm not. Not letting go of my marriage, my pain, and now my closest friend. A portion of his ashes are mailed to me; I stand alone on the edge of my concrete deck, opening the lid of the small wooden urn while gazing at pink, misty mountains shimmering beneath a soft morning sky. Whisper a prayer on the steady breeze and toss his remains. A moment later, caught by the light wind, they blow back in my face. Up my nose, into my mouth, my eyes. I'm covered.

If he's watching; he's laughing at the irony.

I'm crying… For him. For me. For everything there is, and everything that's gone.

Something has to give; it's my health.

It takes only a few weeks for my bodyweight to plummet from a hundred and seventy-four to one hundred and fifty-seven pounds. The strange stiffness in my shoulders turns to pain, migrates to my hips and becomes so excruciating that I can barely walk, and sleep is all but impossible. A look in my bedroom mirror brings shock. Muscles soft and shrunken, skin hanging in flaps, face drawn and lined. Pride, vanity, all gone in a flood of fear and self-pity.

I turn away, unable to accept the man staring back at me. Certain I have cancer. What else can explain the terrible pain and the rapid loss of weight?

A trip to the lab. Hobbling painfully from the car to the waiting room.

A blood test reveals that an autoimmune disease, not cancer, is the problem; then a consultation with a rheumatologist. She tells me that I'm lucky, this particular disease, polymyalgia rheumatica, lasts an average of three years, but it can as easily be a lifetime. No one knows. The good news, if there is any, is that it will not kill me. Three years? A lifetime? I'm not going to spend a lifetime, or even three years, living like this, or taking prednisone to suppress my immune system with all its side effects, from weight gain to high blood pressure. No, that is not for me.

And that's when the fighter rears his head, and all the things that I have studied and practiced since I was a teenager — progressive resistance exercise, martial arts, yoga and meditation — come to save me. Exercise of my body and mind, low doses of anti-inflammatory drugs … and prayer.

***

~4~

Seven months later; months in which I am vulnerable, scared and raw, yet months in which I continue to exercise, meditate and pray, allowing myself the time and space to heal. Inflammation levels return to normal. No more pain. The doctor calls me a miracle. No more drugs. No more weekly blood draws. The disease has vanished. I'm officially well... Physically, anyway.

Time passes.

Papers are filed with the county court. We sell the house, another tough exercise in letting go, and divide the assets according to California law, a fifty-fifty split, leaving me with a lot less than I had anticipated or hoped for in my "golden" years.

The divorce is final.

Leaving one more thing in need of closure, and for that I go to a friend, who is also an established psychiatrist. Once a pitcher for a professional baseball team; he's tall, lean, and handsome in a blond, square-jawed heroic kind of way; and more than a decade older than I am, which makes me feel comfortable since I trust life experience more than classroom knowledge. Compassion spills from his wide blue eyes and wisdom from his lips. No psychobabble or new-age platitudes; I feel as if I am in the presence of a tribal elder with my classical dilemma, how to mend a broken heart.

I talk, he listens, first about Michelle, whose name he jots down on his yellow legal pad, and then about some of my other, more recent, forays into singledom, and, finally, about my ex-wife; which is the real reason I'm here.

Towards the end of the hour, he asks, "Why do you think she wanted the divorce?"

I pause and consider his question, the same question I asked her years ago, over and over again, and could never get an answer. But now, with time, distance, and a more relaxed communication between us, we've talked about it.

"She said I was too controlling."

"Were you?"

"Probably, but I wasn't aware of it, not at the time ... It was my world, and she went along with it."

"Your world?"

"Moving from England to New York, then out here. It was all my idea. Trying to set projects up in Hollywood, turn my books into films. Write screenplays. There were a lot of close calls, lots of options, but no real success. I think that made a difference to her."

"Why?"

"I wasn't the great provider she'd hoped for. Maybe she lost respect for me."

"Is there an age gap between you?"

"Nineteen years," I answer. Remembering that when our relationship began, I commented that when I was twenty, she would have been a one-year-old; I could have changed her diapers. She laughed and answered that she'd probably end up changing mine. I thought it was funny at the time, now I'm not so sure.

The Elder sits in silence. Looking at me, seated on the sofa, going to places I don't want to go.

"She said she felt numb, had no identity, no self-esteem," I continue. "And then, there was the money. The new house was eating it up, and I wasn't exactly setting the film world on fire. She's got a thing about financial security and we were losing ours, nail by nail." I lower my head, sorrow dragging me down. "We only spoke about this stuff recently ... If we'd have talked when it was happening, maybe we could have worked on it ..."

"How did you feel when she abandoned you?"

His question brings back a flood of emotion. Abandoned? The word is a spark.

"Angry," I answer, feeling the fire. "Very angry."

"Why?"

"Because she wouldn't talk. Whenever I asked why she was acting the way she was, she always answered, "I don't know." She kept saying, "I don't know … It drove me nuts.""

"I understand … That's very frustrating."

I struggle to squeeze my feelings into words. They come out flat.

"She didn't want me anymore."

The Elder's voice is quiet, considered.

"Are you still in love with her?"

I feel tears welling.

"I still feel something, just not sure what it is."

Pass me the Kleenex. Here they come.

"Those feelings are natural," he says.

The hour ends, and life goes on.

*

I find a small but charming place on the East End of town, a sanctuary amongst the orange groves, while my ex-wife buys and begins renovation on a place near the center. She intends to move to either London, where she grew up, or Los Angeles, when our youngest son finishes high school. The oldest has already left the nest, with a full scholarship to play tennis at a private college up North.

There is no turning back, and I am experiencing a new kind of loneliness, different than the solitary bedroom on the mountaintop, with the wife down the hall and the kids in their bedrooms. Now it's a solitary house with empty rooms and no visible neighbors; there is an extraordinary stillness. The night skies are big and blanketed with stars. Friends tell me how lucky I am to live in such peaceful surrounds. They're right, but the peace comes with a price, a sense of isolation.

I realize that I am afraid to be alone. Too much time on my hands, time to think and ponder all the what ifs of my life and create scenarios of what will be, all the while trying to shed the skin of my old self as a new self struggles to emerge.

There is a distinct finality to waking up alone, spending days alone, going to bed alone. To driving home alone, with no one at the other end of the road. Entering an empty house. Alone.

I've been married twice, each for eighteen years, and alone is not a place I've ever lived.

Alone is asking me to make friends with the silence, and I'm having a hard time with that; my inner voice continues to try to fill the void with the same old story. Why did this happen? Why now, at this age? Could I have prevented it? The same old story. What will become of me? Another voice counters with "live in the moment, be here now." All the sixties platitudes, all true, and all so damn hard to live.

My youngest boy spends the weekends with me, and I continue to be on good terms with my ex, visiting her frequently for cups of Argentinian tea and discussions about our new lives, our sons, but sometimes, often, I dread the drive back up the long straight road to my house, particularly when darkness falls.

I'd like a companion. There must be someone out there for me, someone lying alone in a bed at night, someone who would just love a guy like me, whoever that guy might be, but how do I find her? And how does she find me? How do I find me?

*

"Do you go to bars at night?" a friend asks. He is also our lawyer and was instrumental in the sale of our property, the dream house.

"No, never," I answer, admiring the view from the panoramic windows of his Westlake office.

"Then how are you ever going to meet a woman?"

Madam Ann assures me that she's still on the lookout, scouring her Rolodex for ex-starlets, most of them, presumably, still alive, but I'm not holding my breath. So… how *do* I meet a woman? The simple answer is, I don't know; but, before I can say this, there's a ping from the lawyer's computer. He looks down at the blue screen and smiles confidently.

"I've got two dates this weekend."

My lawyer is also going through a divorce, but he has obviously taken some defensive action.

"Take a look at this," he says, motioning me over to his desk. I forsake my mountain views for the image on his screen, blue-eyed and blonde with high prominent cheekbones, full lips cocked in a tempting smile; she looks like a Russian model, the kind that tell you they love you from eight thousand miles away, then ask for plane fare to come visit; and that's the last you see of your money or the Russian model, who is more likely a guy from Ghana.

"Beautiful," I say, keeping the skepticism from my voice.

"Saturday night," he answers.

"Is she local?" I ask, zeroing in. Honey Blond is the name printed beneath the photo and Thousand Oaks appears below, which makes Honey Blond about three miles away. Maybe this is for real.

My lawyer is in his mid-fifties and Honey Blond is thirty-eight, or so her profile reads; I quickly calibrate my sixty-seven years and arrive at my own version of Honey Blond in her late forties. Problem is, I have never done online dating and don't have a clue how it works. Consequently, my lawyer becomes my online mentor.

"I'm on three dating sites," he says. "Probably average at least one date a week. It can be expensive if you take them to dinner, but sometimes I get lucky."

I perk up.

"You need to get online," he says authoritatively. I'm wondering if he's billing me for this advice. "I'll give you a list of dating sites," he continues.

List in hand, I leave his office and drive back to my sanctuary, and the sound of silence. Sit down at my computer, google the site that my lawyer claims to be the most active and begin to apply for membership, all the while envisioning my very own Honey Blond, sitting in front of my fireplace, sipping wine and telling me she loves me. Half an hour later I am frustrated by the amount of questions the site wants me to answer — education, favorite places, favorite books, films and on and on —- and quit.

Finally, my friend Jane steps in; she's an ex-model, ex-actress and currently a successful interior designer, lives in Santa Barbara, is about my age, and has been dating online for two years, a veteran as far as I am concerned. Never a lover but always an ally, we've tried to help each other navigate the quagmire of finding love past sixty. Meeting every Sunday morning at a seaside restaurant, while sharing tales of heartbreaks, triumphs and disappointments over bowls of oatmeal. It's our small and private lonely-hearts club.

Jane has a forty-three-year-old daughter, Samantha, who, she explains, met her husband online, a fact that adds credibility to the possibility of lasting cyber-love. Giving me hope. Then promises that she and Samantha will sit down with me and guide me through the registration process.

Finding love has now become a priority. I know it's out there; I've just got to get to it. Somehow, I've convinced myself that once that happens, all the other aspects of my life will fall into place, like magic.

I set a date with Jane and Samantha to begin the process.

But ... before I do, I consult the Tribal Elder, my friend who is now my psychiatrist, and explain my plans for finding the right person through the internet. He listens. I rationalize, using my lawyer's logic, that since I don't sit on a barstool drinking wine at any of the local places or attend cocktail parties where I might meet new female friends, the only chance I have of finding love, now that Ann and her parrot are on hiatus, is in cyberspace. He nods his head and makes notes on his legal pad, glancing up at me whenever my flow of words falters. Encouraging me onwards with a few more nods of his head. Strangely, his yellow legal pad begins to stir memories of the one I used to figure out my net worth prior to the division of assets. Not a happy recollection.

"So, what do you think?" I ask.

"What do *you* think?" He returns my question with a sagely twist of tone, turning my question into his question.

"About all this online stuff. Do you think I'll find someone?" I continue.

"I think you should spend more time alone, learning to love yourself."

"I spend a lot of time alone," I answer.

"What does it feel like?"

"Lonely."

"Does it hurt?"

"Yes, I worry that I'll always be alone."

"What does the hurt feel like?"

"Like a hollow in my gut. Some kind of deep sorrow for what might have been."

"And what might have been?" he asks.

"A happy marriage. A happy family. A happy house on the mountain."

His eyes well up, as if he can feel my pain.

"Let it go," he soothes.

"It leaves a void inside me," I say.

"Live in that void for a while. Feel it. Learn from it."

"Do you believe I'll ever find anybody to fill it up?"

"Yes." He pauses, holding my eyes. "You," he adds.

We conclude the session with a restorative handshake followed by a warm embrace, and I'm gone. To Santa Barbara.

Jane and her daughter, Samantha, await.

Sitting me down at the dining table. Switching on the computer and accessing the "most active" dating site, and, here they come again, those tedious questions that stalled my last attempt.   Samantha takes over the keyboard as I stumble through the "profile" section, trying to avoid hyperbole, while Jane cheerleads from the sidelines. Finally, it comes to my date of birth. I spit out the year; it sounds like a confession. Samantha takes her hands from the keyboard and stares across at me as if I am a rusted relic from an archeological dig.

"You are not going to put that down," she says.

"No, you can't do that," Jane adds, hovering above the screen.

"But ..."

"Fifty-nine. You're going to be fifty-nine."

"But I'm sixty-seven," I say. "Nearly sixty-eight."

"That's too tough an age. Too close to seventy. You're going to limit your options."

"What happens when they meet me?"

"Everybody does it, trust me," Samantha says. "Besides, you look great ... for your age." Which feels like the equivalent of someone calling me "young man" at the supermarket, then asking if I need help carrying my groceries to the car.

I look up at Jane. She nods her head. "I lied by a few years," she confirms.

"How many?"

"Ten," she answers.

That does it for me. If Oatmeal Jane, one of the most honest people I've ever met, needed to fib, I'll do it too.

"Okay," I agree. On top of which, the main photo we are using is already seven years old; the smile may be the same, but in real life the burgeoning turkey neck may give me away. Age, it's always in the neck. I'll keep smiling and trust my charm to pull me through.

A half hour later and I've got a full profile, including a brief biography, stressing sensitive assets like my guitar playing and reading books by Herman Hesse. That, plus five photos in various states of happy times and wide smiles and I'm ready for the love of my life. It feels elating.

I choose the six-month option, pay with my credit card, thank Jane and Samantha and send a silent prayer to the Cyber-Gods.

Before I leave, Samantha says, "You'll probably get a lot of response in the first few days because you're new on the site, that's the way it works. Have fun!"

*

My first stop the following morning is to my computer which sits on the desk of my office. I sit down, type in the password and hit the postage stamp icon for mail. Excitement builds as I see four messages from the dating site. Samantha was right; I've got action. Open the first, which transfers me to the message, "Hi Richard, nice profile," and a thumbnail-sized photo of the sender. Frizzy hair, panoramic smile, and big sunglasses. Not much visible face. And no gut reaction from me. Then I go straight to the site. Seven "likes," which lifts my spirits. There's nothing like a little hope in the midst of despair, during those times when we feel that everything good has deserted us, never to return. Then I read the other messages, a couple of "hellos," which I interpret as openings for me to say hello back and build a conversation, and one lady who tells me she likes my profile and that we have things in common. She's riding a horse in her profile picture, wearing a helmet and wielding a riding crop with a look on her face that suggests she means business, and since I've been on a horse maybe five times in my life, I cannot imagine what we have in common. Unless, of course, she thinks I may be into a little S & M and intends to use the crop on me.

Finally, there's one photo that catches my eyes: English Rose, a sandy-haired lady with wonderful green eyes, perfect pert nose and kissable lips, my very own version of Honey Blond. Her message is thoughtful, "Hello Richard. Loved your profile. I am a university professor with a PhD in literature. I see you are a writer; would I know of any of your books?" It all sounds a bit highbrow and I doubt that an English professor would have read my motorcycle memoirs or martial arts-based thrillers, but you never know. English Rose ends her message by suggesting a phone call and asking for my number.

Suddenly, the long driveway that leads from my office window to the private road at the bottom and the trees beyond that has lately seemed, particularly on rainy days, a long, lonely road to the great void, becomes a magical path to new love and adventure.

So, this is how it's done.

English Rose.

I message her back, give her my phone number, and suggest a time for the call. Tonight. Seven o'clock. Why wait?

She agrees and promises to phone.

I am very excited; in fact, so excited that it's hard to think of anything else all day. It may sound silly, a man nudging seventy with the hopes of an adolescent, but life lately has become an emotional roller-coaster. I'm down one moment and flying high the next; although I admit that the downs vastly outweigh the highs, and the highs are generally based upon appointments with my shrink, who assures me that I am growing from this experience and that with time I will emerge whole again, or maybe whole for the first time in my life. He also jots down the names of every woman that I claim an interest in on his legal pad, slowly accumulating a list equivalent to Madam Ann's. I wonder why he is doing this. All in all, I'm a long way from anywhere, but sometimes when we are stranded in limbo, we, mercifully, don't know it.

I even dress up for my phone date, jeans and clean shirt, casual and comfortable, as if English Rose can actually see me. Pour a glass of red wine, light a fire. Seven o'clock and the phone does not ring. I'm okay with this, so far, but by seven-twenty I have finished my wine and am headed for another glass. Can't believe this is happening.

Then, midway through my pour, it rings; I give it a few before I answer.

"Richard?"

"Yes?"

"This is Sarah."

"As in English Rose?" I ask.

"The same." Before I can say more, she adds, "I'm sorry I'm late, but my last class ran over and I literally just walked through the door."

I tell her that I forgive her, and the real conversation begins, covering everything from our mutual appreciation for the 19th century English poet and writer D. H. Lawrence to the fact that she rides a Harley, an old obsession of mine, and used to practice power lifting in the gym, which is Olympic style weightlifting and consists of using maximal weight in three tough lifts. Seems unusual for a woman, let alone an English professor, and is very hardcore compared to the yoga and aerobics that most of the women on the dating site claim to practice. We go on for two hours, concluding with an invitation to share a bottle of champagne at her house on Friday evening, which is only a day away. I ask her to text me her address, promise to bring the champagne and the call ends.

She texts. We're on.

Sleep comes in spurts. All I can think of is English Rose, with her gorgeous green eyes and Harley Davidson motorcycle, riding through my overactive imagination. Surely, this is all meant to be. Even the break-up of my marriage rings with a certain poetry. This is my life, my new life. What could be sweeter?

Morning comes and as soon as the wine store opens, I'm in. Dom Perignon seems pretentious and it's very expensive, so I settle on a bottle of Veuve Clicquot, an old favorite from my days in London. Light and crisp and coming in at just under $60, it's slightly less common than Moet and doesn't look like I'm trying to impress. I take it home and stick it in the refrigerator. Sit down at my desk and attempt to begin a new book, something I've been trying to do for months, generally stalling at the second page. I've begun writing four books so far in as any months and abandoned all of them. My agent is becoming uncertain if I'll ever write again. "Send me fifty pages," he says, as I sit and stare at the empty screen. It feels like he's suggesting I climb Mt. Everest wearing nothing but a Speedo. It's either stare at the blue screen or stare out the window down the long driveway that formerly led to a lonely oblivion but now leads to English Rose. Naturally, I prefer English Rose. Finally, darkness falls.

Do I sleep?

Not a chance.

I remain awake most of the night, occasionally turning to check the time on the digital clock on my bedside table. I really want to look fresh and rested, youthful, for this first meeting but now, if I get a few hours I'll be happy.

I have a vivid dream. Featuring my ex-wife. She's riding along a tree-lined street on a bicycle. I am following behind, peddling furiously, trying to catch up; she takes a fast turn down a side road and I'm headed headlong into a tree. I wake up. Making a mental note to write this dream down and present it at my next therapy session. It must mean something profound, but at 4:30 AM with English Rose on the horizon I don't worry about dream interpretations.

I toss and turn.

*

Up at six and into my sweats for a workout at the gym; I'm feeling very energized in spite of the fact that I have not slept much. The adrenaline is flowing and I'm counting the hours till I leave to meet Sarah, otherwise known as English Rose. She has given me an address in The Pacific Palisades, which is a rich Los Angeles community that lies between the Santa Monica Mountains and the Pacific Ocean, about seventy miles or an hour and a half from me, maybe two, depending on traffic. She has also provided two entrance codes for the security gates that protect her property.

Judging by her address and the double security codes, English Rose appears to be an incredibly successful English professor; or maybe the money is from her last divorce, or the two divorces before that she mentioned on the phone, and I'm thinking that perhaps I should have bought the Dom Perignon. I'm also wondering why she's been married and divorced three times but then look at myself, the veteran of two divorces, and think it's best not to be judgmental; there are reasons for everything.

The day passes with the writing of several paragraphs of a new thriller that I eventually delete because none of it makes much sense, on top of which I'm only going through the motions, passing time, till I l leave for my destined meeting in The Palisades.

English Rose and I have agreed to meet at five to pop the cork, so I give myself two and a half hours, preferring to get to her neighborhood early and have a cup of coffee somewhere local than be caught in traffic cursing and sweating.

At two o'clock I begin preparations. A second shower, a second shave, the finger-comb, a careful examination of all possible clothing combinations, deciding on black jeans and a green cotton shirt. Light on the cologne and to the fridge to retrieve the Clicquot. Into the car, plugging The Palisades address into the navigation system before rolling down the long driveway on my way to what I hope is the beginning of the rest of my life. Listening to Bruce Springsteen's "Dancing In The Dark" on the radio. "You can't start a fire without a spark," Bruce sings. "This gun's for hire ..." I add, "Even if it's a flintlock."

***

~5~

There's money in California, lots of money, and the Malibu traffic nudging along at ten miles an hour gives me plenty of pause to look at the line-up of multimillion-dollar houses that literally sit on the road with their porched fronts looking out at the blue-gray ocean. I can't help but wonder how the occupants back out of their garages and on to the busy highway without a collision and why anyone would pay millions to live like this. Glad I left early, more concerned now with timing than what awaits on the other end of the road. The navigation says I am less than five miles from my destination in The Palisades, and it's just nudging four-thirty on the clock so I should be just about on time.

Yes, I'm nervous and no matter how many times I tell myself that this is just another online date, rationalizing that I have never actually met the lady and that I am not a kid, it doesn't feel that way. This feels very important, like life or death important. The reason for this is simple: I am lonely, just like the other millions of single adults past the age of forty-five or the thirty percent of people over sixty-five that live in one-person households, struggling for relevance in a techno-world that moves like lightning, passing them by. I'm just like everyone else, everyone I see on the dating sites and the Facebook pages. Looking for love. It can be frightening, with feelings of isolation and depression. Growing old gracefully is much easier said than done. I want someone to enter and fill the void I feel when I sit at my desk and stare down the driveway or lay in my bed and wonder if there will ever be another warm body beside me, someone to talk to before I sleep. At times, I struggle to prevent feelings of hopelessness from dominating me, but they are there, lurking.

"Fill the void with yourself. Learn to be your own best friend. Love yourself. Appreciate solitude. Climb Mt. Everest in a Speedo."

These are the thoughts I am having as my Chevrolet Volt, with a bottle of champagne chilling the passenger seat, creeps down the PCH en route to a house locked behind security gates and a woman I have never met, who claims to be forty-nine, posts only head shots on the dating site, told me she looks so alluring in a swimsuit that she is self-conscious on the beach; a woman who is about to be visited by a sixty-seven-year-old man who claims to be a year shy of sixty.

Let the games begin.

It's four-forty-five when I pull off the main drag and onto a private road that leads to the first iron gate. Fifteen minutes to spare, which is just as well since I cannot find the piece of paper with the security codes written on it. Thought I had it in my pocket, but no matter how deep I dig I can't find it. Did I leave it on the kitchen table? I sit and try to remember. Pull out both pockets. Nothing. Okay. I must have her phone number in my cell phone. But no, I don't have that either, because I felt more at ease using the big handset of my landline, so I'm screwed. There's no entry phone attached to the gate. I'm desperate. Frustrated to the point of screaming curses at the sky. Feeling like a complete idiot. Sitting outside her gate with no way in and no way to tell her I'm out here … unless … I climb the gate, which appears to be about seven feet high. I park the car on the side of the road and get out. Survey the iron fortress. Hoping like hell she doesn't have armed security. There don't seem to be any cameras, so I wrap my hands around the upper bars, getting a good grip. Luckily, I train regularly and do pull-ups. Should be able to get over it; the champagne can wait. Hopefully, English Rose will have a sense of humor. Maybe my Commando style entrance will make her laugh, or somehow impress her. Certainly, more than a no-show or an explanatory call from my house, two hours back up the highway. Then, after the laughter that I hope will accompany my entrance, we can come back and retrieve my car, and the champagne. It's going to be a forced entry; there's no other way. I pull my body up, trying to wedge my suede boot onto the next bar on the gate, fitting my cushioned toe snugly between the railings. One more heave and I should be able to lift a leg over the top. Hopefully, I won't impale myself and be found dangling by my fly front. About to execute the big push when I hear the crunch of tires against gravel. Maybe she does have armed security. I freeze, like a spider in a web. It's an older SUV, maybe fifty yards away. Before I'm spotted, I drop from the gate and hustle back to my car. Get in and start it up. The SUV, an older Volvo, pulls closer and stops; the gate slowly opens. I can see a silver-haired Hispanic lady behind the wheel.

She stares at me.

I smile and wave.

She smiles back.

I throw the Volt into Drive, pull forward till I'm beside her, driver side to driver's side, and lower my window. Looks like cleaning materials in the back of her Volvo, mops and brooms, a vacuum cleaner, rags. I assume she works for English Rose.

We are now parallel, and the gate is open when I motion with my hand for her to lower her window. She does.

"I've come to see Sarah," I say.

She doesn't appear to understand me, so I give her my full range of Spanish.

"Sarah aqui?"

"In house," Volvo answers; her English an equivalent to my Spanish.

"Ahora?"

"Yes, now."

"Gracias," I reply, waving a casual goodbye as I slide the Volt through the opened gate.

Lucky me, the second one has an entry phone. No climbing required; I press the button.

A female voice crackles, "You're right on time." Followed by a buzz. This gate opens onto a large courtyard, complete with several fountains and a life-sized statue of the naked David, by Michelangelo. A wide-paved walkway leads to the ten-foot-high entrance doors of the Rose residence.

The house is big and new, a McMansion, pretentious in its grandeur.

I'm nervous as, grasping the bottle of Clicquot in my left hand, I ring the entrance buzzer with my right. Another few anxious seconds to wonder what happens next and the door opens.

"Richard?"

This person bears no resemblance to the photos that I've seen online. I'm talking none. She is very short and very wide, and not in the muscular, power lifting sense of the word. It has obviously been a long time since she's seen the gym. Her hair is not sandy blonde; it's fiery red, in tune with her bright painted lips.

"Sarah?" I ask, almost expecting her to step aside to reveal the true English Rose.

"Were you expecting someone else?" she answers with a smile that reveals a full set of ultra-white veneers.

I'm in trouble before I even set foot inside. This is not what I had in mind, nothing like it, but in I go, following English Rose, who doesn't look or sound at all English, more Jewish or maybe Italian, down a long, tiled corridor that is lined with various pieces of sculpture, ceramics, and art sitting on long tables or hanging on the walls. There is a bronze face mask within range, and without thought, or maybe because I'm so ill at ease and need something to do, I reach out and touch it with my fingertips.

"Don't touch anything," Rose snaps. "If we're going to have a relationship, you're going to have to learn to respect art. That piece you just manhandled is an original Brancusi."

Suitably chastened, I withdraw my offending fingers and follow her lamely to a room adjoining the kitchen. There's a long white sofa in the corner of the room.

"We can sit right there," she says, her voice softer, indicating the sofa.

I'm still in a state of mild shock and haven't spoken, just following orders. I sit and she sits down beside me, finally noticing the bottle of champagne in my hand.

"Thank you," she says, removing it from my grasp. "I'll keep it cold till the guests arrive."

"Guests?" I repeat.

"Yes. Thought I'd have a small party to introduce you, just a few close friends, but they won't be here for an hour." With that she gets up; I presume it's to put the champagne on ice.

I am about to offer a minor protest about meeting her friends so soon, about to say that I have another appointment in an hour, about to bolt for the door when I notice that the edge of her blue polka-dot skirt has lodged in her panty hose, and as she turns her entire rear end is staring me in the face. It's a formidable sight.

"Excuse me," I say, trying to insert a touch of humor while sparing Rose any unnecessary embarrassment, "but your skirt has malfunctioned and I'm staring at your rear end."

She reaches back and rubs her hand over her hind quarters, large, round and sleek through the tight fabric, making no attempt to dislodge her skirt.

"Well ... Do you like what you see?"

Actually, not at all, so I choose silence as my response.

"All right, all right," she grumbles as she frees the polka-dots, dropping the curtain on the nylon Mona Lisa, before opening the fridge to deposit the Clicquot beside several other bottles, probably Dom.

After that, and dispensing with any trivial chit-chat, it's down to business. What type of drugs do I prefer when having sex? While I ponder a reply, she lets me know that she likes a blend of opiates, particularly an exquisite mix of the downers Oxycontin and Norco, both highly addictive, with an occasional snort of crushed Adderall, an amphetamine with euphoric properties, to top it off and balance out the sedative properties of the first two. The Adderall usually gets the party started, although she advises that sometimes the "Addies" require a little Viagra to help maintain enthusiasm in the lower, less cerebral regions. She tells me all these things with a straight face and sincere tone. Perhaps she is a fan of my biker memoirs. I've probably been recruited. A college professor, really? I ask this question discreetly, phrasing it a way that does not hint of skepticism. She answers in the affirmative, citing a well-known and well-respected university which is within a few miles of her McMansion. As I listen, l am planning my escape route. I definitely do not want to have sex with Panty Hose, formerly known as English Rose, or any of her friends. She inches a little closer on the sofa, then tells me the house and the priceless art that she has collected over the years come via her latest ex-husband who was a very successful plastic surgeon in Beverly Hills.

She shifts to full profile, and asks if I like her nose, which is courtesy of the ex and should qualify, according to her, to join the other pieces that line the corridor leading to the white sofa. Which explains the "pert" nose that features in the smiling shots of English Rose. I wonder what it looked like before. And the lips, all puffy and full? The ex? Before I get to the lips she turns suddenly and kisses me on the mouth, inserting her tongue, big and rubbery and feels like it's halfway down my throat. I'm gagging, thinking of scenes from *Alien* and pushing away. She's strong; and I recall her description as a power lifter. I'm strong, too, so it becomes a minor wrestling match on the white sofa. She's on top, her panty-hosed posterior flashing the ceiling. Finally, dredging up some of my old martial art skills, I break the clinch, push away and back off. Thankfully, her tongue slides from my throat and remains in her mouth.

"You're a good kisser," she says.

To my knowledge I was not a participant in the kiss, unless gagging qualifies me.

God knows what comes next. Then, there's the prospect of her close friends. Due any time. Will they be male, female, or something in-between? I will be outnumbered, possibly overwhelmed. Tied up, stripped naked, wrapped in panty hose, fed opiates, stimulated with Adderall, and plied with large doses of Viagra. I've got to get out of here. Now.

"So, what do you think?" she asks.

"About what?"

"Us," she says matter-of-factly.

Not a chance, I think, but don't want to incur her wrath, so I go with a gentler, "I don't really know you."

"Do you want to?"

Now she's pushing it and I sense it's time to make a move, before she chokes me with another kiss. I stand up. She appears puzzled.

"Going somewhere?" she asks.

"I've got to get back home," I reply.

"But… What about the champagne?"

"Share it with your friends, please," I answer.

"So … that's it?" she asks. "You're leaving before my friends arrive."

"Yes, I really have to."

"Will I see you again?"

"I don't think so."

That's it.

She stands up. Almost as if she were expecting this. Everything has gone a bit flat, as if we've been watching a film in color. Now, it's all in black and white.

"Then ... let me walk you to your car," she says.

We walk silently down the art-lined corridor, past the original Brancusi, now sullied by my fingerprints, and to the massive front doors. She opens one and, silently, we head towards the Volt.

I click my remote and the door locks snap open. Have my hand on the handle when she touches my shoulder. I turn.

"Not even gonna' kiss me goodbye?" Resignation in her tone.

I offer my lips, and she kisses me without any aggression and minus her tongue. Then I'm into the car and away. Feeling as though I am making an escape from Alcatraz. Through the first gate, then the second, which is the one I was going to climb an hour ago, when I was full to the brim with hope and expectation and my bottle of champagne was riding confidently beside me. I hit the Pacific Coast Highway, take a right turn and my spirits soar; I sense a certain freedom, even have a quiet laugh as I recall my latest romantic escapade and know that it will make a great story to tell my friends, particularly those who, like me, are looking for a connection online. The laughter lingers in my mind till I hit the long, curving highway on the northside of Malibu; the lights of town are now behind me, the rolling surf of the great gray Pacific swells and settles to my left and the crescent moon and silver stars float above, lighting the highway ahead, leading me to a melancholia that I am all too familiar with. I suddenly feel sorry for myself; then I feel sorry for English Rose. Finding love is not an easy path, and we all travel it in our own way. What would the Elder say? "Love yourself, first; the rest will follow." But how do I do that?

***

~6~

My experience with English Rose sets me back; I become a little gun shy regarding wanting to meet another woman online, wondering how many of them are true to their self-descriptions and ten-year-old photographs. I'd better not pass judgement; after all, thanks to Jane's daughter and my own fear and vanity, I, too, am a serious offender in the age department. I attempt to re-evaluate my addictive need for this cyber-dating. Why can't I just run into to a beautiful single woman in the aisle of Trader Joe's and call it a day, or call it a relationship? Why is there no one local? The answer to that is that I live in a town of eight thousand people; we don't have a Trader Joe's, and I've probably seen or shared a lap lane in the local swimming pool with all the single women in my age range, prior to shedding eight online years and becoming fifty-nine again, and, so far, no luck. This is more like Alaska and a mail-order bride. Have lonely heart, will travel.

Even from my limited experience I've learned that online dating is a numbers game, and it takes a lot of time and energy to play; not to mention belief, faith and the money and old-fashioned chivalry required to drive a hundred miles, pay for dinner and wine when you know within seconds that you have zero in common with your online match and will probably never see this person again. But, as my lawyer-mentor astutely pointed out, "What's the alternative?" However, he has recently augmented his teachings with another slice of wisdom, "Just meet for a cup of coffee." Acquired after his thirty-third online date and a maxed-out credit card.

I visit the Tribal Elder and take my place on his red velvet sofa, facing him. There's compassion in his eyes as he adds English

Rose, below Michelle and the names of several local ladies, to his list of failed potential partners, reminding me of the build-ups and the let-downs, the ebb and the flow, over and over again. Finally, the Elder suggests that I give up the entire dating process for a month, taking time out to delve deeper into my inner psyche. I should sit at home in my favorite chair, arms outspread, welcoming the feelings of loneliness, hopelessness, and quiet desperation, or ... generally feeling that all is lost ... until these feelings dissipate, wash over and pass through me as I learn to recognize their impermanence. "Let go, just let go," he coaxes. Nothing lasts forever. Sounds like meditation to me.

I tell him I will, but I know I won't. An addict is an addict, and I am now addicted to the dating site. Continuing to check my computer for "views," "likes" and the much-heralded "message" every morning before I settle into my avocado on toast and drink my coffee with almond milk. There is always a prayer, a spark and a promise. We are creatures of habit, and online dating, or online checking to see who likes me and who I like, have become part of my habits. In fact, on many mornings, before I have so much as a glass of water, I sit down and tune in to the dating site, hoping against hope that the woman of my dreams will be staring back at me from the screen, with a "like" beside her name, and perhaps, if I am extremely lucky, a "message." Waiting for *the magical other*.

Time passes.

A few dates, long drives, more money on the credit card, nothing special.

And then one morning it happens, or I think it happens. There is a "message," and it reads like no other message I've had to date; in other words, it is lengthy and considered, not the usual feelers, the hi's and hello's, like bait on a hook. This one gets right into it, as the sender, code name Seeker, describes herself as a fifty-year-old woman who is divorced, was born in Florida, lived in Santa Barbara for twenty years, created her own business in organic products, sold it to pursue a more isolated and spiritual path in Taos, New Mexico, and now wants to return to California to live this section of her life with a spiritually attuned partner. She's interested in the same books that interest me, including *The Four Agreements*, which I've recently read and found to possess four great universal truths, if only we had the depth and discipline to adhere to them. The first truth is "be impeccable with your words." In other words, don't lie, don't pass judgement on yourself or others, don't criticize, and remain compassionate to yourself and others. Words that are easier said, or read, than done. Still, it's a simple, beautiful book, and holding true to "The Agreements" can be very testing in the online meat market: "Hello, my name's Richard, I'm fifty-nine."

Only problem with The Seeker's correspondence is that she does not include a photograph of herself; there is not a single picture on the site, simply a round vacant circle where her face should be. God, I can only imagine the beauty, or the horror. Then she writes, in her personal message to me, that if I'd like to see photos, I should send her my email address. My immediate thoughts are that this is a scam. Playing on my lonely heart. The man from Ghana? Then, I remember my recent escapade with English Rose, the lady who was too frightened to present her perfect body on a public beach, with or without pantyhose, and wonder whose pictures she used on the site and what does it matter anyway since most people's pictures are at least as old as mine? Let's face it, there is no real way to get the sense of another person other than a face-to-face meeting, and even then, it's difficult. Maybe we should all cut to the chase, get married for a trial run of two years and see how it works out.

I send my email address and hope for the best.

One day. Two. Three. A quiet desperation settles like the forlorn mist at the end of my driveway, then, when I have all but given up, "ping," and there it is, the long-awaited email from Taos.

By any standards, the Seeker is beautiful. If I have a type, she is it; although I probably share this attraction with a hundred thousand other guys in cyberspace, or at least the ones who have seen this photograph. Long, dark hair, brown, soulful eyes and full lips. There's something American Indian about her features. High cheekbones, oval shaped face and angular jawline. She's dressed in a casual but sophisticated style with an open, button-front blue sweater, and a delicate gold necklace. No wonder she doesn't post this photo; her computer would be jammed with admirers. She seems too good to be true. And maybe she is. Is this actually The Seeker or a photoshopped copy of a fashion model from *Vogue*? Hello Ghana.

*

At moments like these, when hope, no matter how true or false, was returned to my broken heart, an incredible euphoria took over, and life, once again, seemed to hold wonder. Thoughts of old age, arthritic knees, fading vision, unwanted solitude and solo Saturday nights vanished as the winter of my discontent morphed into a glorious fragrant Springtime. The scent of orange blossoms filled the air. I was young again.

Hello, Seeker. It's me.

*

The Seeker's telephone voice is high and rather girlish, not the wisdom-laced dulcet tones I had imagined; she's more Scooby Doo than Lara Croft. And the conversation is hardly metaphysical, as we chat for an hour about the climate in Taos; I had no idea that it snowed there, in fact I had no idea where Taos actually is, except in New Mexico, and a vague memory of spending a night there, tripping on LSD and banging brutally on my guitar while, in the early 1970s, I wandered my way across America and into Mexico in search of spiritual enlightenment, resulting in an overnight stay in a Mexican jail, but that's another story. The long-distance call continues, we talk seriously, we laugh, I tell her stories of my past, she tells me of hers, and, eventually, we both decide that a face-to-face meeting is in the cards. She says that she has a job interview in Santa Barbara in three weeks; it's to manage an organic farm and, on impulse, I invite her to stay with me ... in a separate bedroom, of course. I bite my tongue but it's too late. There's a lengthy pause from Taos, and I worry that I just stepped over the line and blew it. I can hear her breathing, so I know she's still there. Then ... She accepts. I can't quite believe it, as the springtime in my soul morphs into a balmy Summer's day, with mint juleps on the veranda.

We agree to talk on the phone at least once a week until we meet, and I promise to pick her up at the airport in Santa Barbara. She says she'll send more photos, just to make sure I recognize her. Please do.

Excited is an understatement.

More photos arrive. Standing knee-deep in the snow. With her dog. Modeling a low-cut dress in front of a mirror. Looks like she has a great body. Call it fate. Call it karma. Call me the luckiest man alive. Call it a soulmate?

*

Meanwhile, I continue to talk to the Tribal Elder on a weekly basis. Tribal elder is an easier way for me to think of him than as my psychiatrist, having grown up in an era that carried a stigma concerning therapists and psychiatrists. If you required emotional support in my dad's day, you were weak and unmanly. Didn't matter that you were a lousy husband, negligent father, unfulfilled at work, and generally pissed off with life but petrified of dying, you bore it with lots of anger, a stiff upper lip, and a Manhattan with a maraschino cherry on top. Numbing the pain while waiting for the final knock-out. Well, here I stand. Weak. Unhappy. Lonely. Lost. A serial online philanderer. Guilty as charged.

As soon as I mention The Seeker's name, which is actually Suzanne, he perks up.

"You have another woman in your life?" he asks, reaching for the legal pad. There have been a couple of quick local flings between major online events, quick and shallow sexual encounters, all of which I've reported to him, so the list is growing.

"You're a lover, not a fighter," he concludes.

I wax-on enthusiastically about Suzanne, recounting our past two conversations and the many things we have in common, including several self-help books we've both read and a composite of psycho-active plants and chemicals we've both ingested. He does not look very impressed and it annoys me. Here I am smiling, laughing, and positive about this new woman in my life and he's sitting there with a poker face, jotting down notes.

Then, abruptly, he asks, "Do you ever have dreams of your ex-wife?"

What? Talk about throwing water on the flames. Dreams? Well, I recall the one that had me wheeling my bicycle headlong towards a giant tree while my ex-wife deftly cornered hers onto a quiet side road and continued peddling, but I believe we discussed that dream a few sessions ago. Interpreting it to mean that I was frightened of navigating my own course after eighteen years of co-piloting.

"Think about it," he says.

I do, and it comes to me. Brief but lucid.

"The other night I dreamt I was kissing her passionately. Then I woke up."

He nods, jots down another note and looks into my eyes. There is that familiar compassion in his.

"You miss that feeling of being loved by someone," he says.

I cannot deny this.

"Take more time with yourself. Love yourself. You are not ready for a new relationship."

Bullshit. I don't want to hear this, not when Suzanne The Seeker is scheduled to appear in six days.

*

~7~

Santa Barbara Airport is small, well-manicured and accessible, a jewel of an airport. Not far from the emerald green lawns and seaside campus of the University of California at Santa Barbara, it's rarely crowded, has plenty of parking space and a very relaxed atmosphere, particularly when compared to the noise, bad air and congestion of LAX.

I arrive at 2 o'clock. Walk in through the big doors and find myself a seat on a bench directly facing the down escalator from arrivals. The Seeker's connecting flight from Los Angeles is scheduled to land here in forty-five minutes.

I have a small bouquet of flowers in my hand and feel like an eighteen-year-old kid, about to present an orchid corsage to my date for the senior prom. Jittery. Excited. A little frightened. Wondering what our first impressions will be. Will she be as pretty as the woman in the photographs? Will my arthritic right knee, stiff from being seated, cause me to limp towards her, flowers extended in a quivering hand? The ancient Romeo … Will I look as old as I am?

The speakers come alive with a sharp click and a female voice announces the arrival of the American Airlines flight from Taos via LA. My heart beats in and out of time to "Hit the Road Jack," which is playing on the airport sound system. This is a young man's game. I hope I don't have a stroke.

The way I am positioned, seated on the bench parallel to and below the escalator, allows for a glimpse of the new arrivals' legs with the full reveal taking place as they descend the steel moving staircase. Every time I see what appears to be the lower half of a female body, in jeans, yoga pants, skirt or slacks, I prepare myself to spring-up, or perform my own version of springing up to greet my guest, which, due to a lifetime of athletic injuries and motorcycle crashes, may lack a bit of spring. Many legs descend, and many times I begin to rise from my seat but, so far, nothing that looks like Suzanne. Did she make the flight? Did she decide against it at the last minute? No, that couldn't happen. She's got a job interview. I am not her main reason for coming. Is my *vibrant floral medley* of spring flowers wilting in my hand? Then ... high suede boots, a dark skirt, a beige sweater, a neck. The head is slowly emerging; it's like watching a birth, or more accurately, a breech birth. Long dark hair, I'm already on my feet. She turns and looks in my direction. I feel my mouth open in a wall-to-wall smile as she alights at the bottom of the escalator.

"Suzanne?"

I extend my hand full of the vibrant medley, an array of orange, pink and yellow flowers. She reaches out and accepts. We hug. My God. "Amazing Grace" plays in the astral regions of my mind, "I was lost, now I'm found."

"Richard."

Not much conversation but a shared euphoria, or maybe it's just mine, which has spread to cover the entire airport in a blissful haze as we go to the carousel and wait for her luggage.

"I really like your looks," I say.

"And I really like yours," she answers.

So far, so good, even though "so far" is all of five minutes, but at least the initial meeting is out of the way and no one is having buyer's remorse, not that I know of, anyway.

She points to a weathered Louis Vuitton travel bag and I swoop forward and grab it.

"That's it," she says. "I travel light."

And off we go, out the door, into the light and on to the great adventure of getting to know who the other person is.

*

After being alone for several years, in the sense of not having an official partner to share the basic patterns of life, it feels strange and somewhat alien to have a female presence in the passenger side of my car. Yes, I've given women rides to events and taken a few out to dinner, but this feels different. I have a beautiful woman sitting next to me, trusting me enough to allow me to take her to my home, and as we travel, I realize that trust is a main component in any kind of relationship. Trust is the glue that holds partners together, and a partner is what I have told myself I am looking for. The mutual physical attraction is important, but after that comes the reality of knowing and accepting another person. Suzanne feels self-assured and confident, and sophisticated in a worldly sense, but I could be anybody, driving her anywhere and she has trusted me to take her home.

We are riding in silence as I connect with the 101 Freeway, yet there feels a certain ease between us, an understanding of sorts. We are both searching for love, or at least that's what we have told each other in emails and texts and on the telephone, but at what level are we able to give or receive it? We are two strangers. Prepared to try each other out, see what works, and what does not. I know my heart is still in disrepair; I can feel it when I wake up in the middle of the night or sit and stare out the window of my office, down the long driveway, thinking about what might have been; I still have dreams of my ex-wife but I have not dared to mention these to Suzanne or any of the other women I have dated, for fear of rejection. I mean, who wants to hear about another person's heartaches? Sitting there, sipping wine or eating food in a restaurant, listening to descriptions and stories of another's unrequited love. Not me. Not anyone I've dated. It's a sure sign that the person is not ready to move on, or has not.

The Elder says I must take time to heal in order to learn to love myself, perhaps for the first time, before I can undertake a commitment to anyone else. To become whole. But I am impatient. I don't want to take time; at 67, I feel as if I don't have much time left. I want to take a short-cut, but I don't think there are any and I don't want to fully own this fact. I cannot ask this person seated beside me to heal me, to make me whole, yet, in a way, isn't that exactly what I am asking her to do? And what does

she need from me? Who am I, and who is Suzanne The Seeker?
What is she seeking?

*

A little talk about her upcoming job interview, a few stabs at humor
regarding my inability to begin a new book, more talk of her intent
to move from Taos and re-establish herself in California and we
are driving through the mountain pass on our way into town. I
think we are both being cautious as to what we say about ourselves.
Choosing our words carefully, as the other is listening for red flags,
or warning signs; anything that suggests the new potential partner
is missing some vital ingredient for a real relationship; maybe too
needy, too desperate, a depressive, or bi-polar, or an absolute
psycho, although a forty-five-minute car ride is hardly enough time
to diagnose a dangerous psychiatric disorder. "It takes at least a
year to get to know someone completely, maybe two," I've been
told time and again by my friend and confidante Ingrid, the yoga
teacher. Well, Ingrid, I don't want to hear it. I don't have two years.
I want it now.
     "But you need to spend time alone, to heal, to become
whole," repeats the Elder.
     Shut up and go back to writing notes on your legal pad or
interpreting dreams. I'm tired of being alone. I'll take a short-cut.
     Left turn into town and only a few miles from my house.
She reaches over and touches my hand with hers, emphasizing
something she's saying. It's a nice touch and Suzanne has beautiful
hands, well-formed with long slender fingers, and warm. I like the
warmth, the human touch. I sense a rush of hope. Maybe I am
healed enough to allow another person inside my heart. Maybe
Suzanne is whole enough to avoid becoming another notation on
the Elder's legal pad.
     Down the long, tree-lined avenue, though the groves of
oranges and left turn into the private road that leads to my
driveway. Right turn ahead. It's a different view going up, towards
the green craftsman style house with the circular gravel drive and
the giant oak tree in the center. The fountain in front of my office
is bubbling, greeting us. It feels so good to be looking up, not

down, and feels good because I am not alone. Right here, right now, I am not alone.

It feels like we are partners as we enter the house, or partners in the making, familiar but still testing the waters; I show Suzanne to her bedroom and leave her alone to change clothes and get comfortable without me hovering around. It's already nearly six and I've booked a restaurant for seven. I go up the winding stairs to my own bedroom and assemble a wardrobe for the evening. It feels strange, somewhat surreal, knowing that there is someone else in the house who is excited for the evening to come, someone who has chosen to come here, to be with me, so far from the rejection of the last years in that dream house on the hill.

The restaurant is quiet, the table lit by two candles. We order a bottle of wine. She looks wonderful, in a black sleeveless dress, deep brown eyes, a white smile, a little cleavage. Yes, I keep glancing at her chest and thinking about sex. What would it be like with Suzanne? Is she as beautiful naked as she is in clothes? I catch myself. I've been focused on her chest for about a minute, has she noticed? Look back into her eyes. Talk about her business in organic foods. Where did she go to school? What do they have on the menu that she will eat? Better watch my step. Don't order meat, not even that turkey meatloaf that I'm so fond of. Don't want to blow this whole thing over a steak? Never. Come on. But be yourself. If you want meat, order it. Don't start this relationship with a lie. Be impeccable with your words.

Dinner ends after two vegetarian lasagnas and two vegan crème brûlées, and the disappearance of the Pinot Noir, with me being the main consumer. Yes, I am now officially a vegan. An intoxicated vegan. In fact, after my second glass I would have become anything necessary to whisk Suzanne back into my car and up that long formerly lonely road to my formerly isolated house. In fact, I was never so happy to have such a quiet place of solitude and meditation, beneath the silver moon and stars amongst the heady orange groves. I'm certain I can drive the three miles without being pulled over and arrested, which would wreck everything, but since this little town closes at about 8 PM, I'm not too worried. Sober enough to run around and open the passenger side door, always the gentleman. We talk, we laugh, we say how good it feels to be together.

Once safely home and in the house behind locked glass doors I suggest another glass of wine and maybe a single hit from the supply of medical marijuana that my oldest son has planted in the back yard. The plants are as high as the roof of my garage, but he has his license and I have an ounce, which covers his rent for the space. She says, yes, and the evening slips into another gear. More chat, more laughter, a little more relaxed, a little kiss that turns into a big kiss. Dim the lights. Oh my God, I'm glad I'm not married.

We wake up together. So nice to wake up beside a human body, instead of the "cuddler," which is the tradename given to the extra-long soft pillow that usually accompanies my sleep, or lack thereof. It's long enough to wrap my legs and arms around, but unfortunately the "cuddler" lacks a head, so there's no chance of a deep conversation, although I've tried.

Suzanne and I talk about her childhood, growing up in Kansas, college in New York, then the big move West, to California, the first state to sell genetically engineered food, which she opposes, but also the state with the most organic farms. Still talking as she gets out of bed and stands in front of me, totally at ease with her naked body, although she comments that if I think her breasts are too saggy, she'll be happy to have them 'done'... if I pay for it. Before I can reassure her that I think her breasts are just fine, she slips into a black silk dressing gown and heads down the stairs. Fifteen minutes later, showered and shaved, I descend and find her reclining in a deck chair on the back porch, taking in a bit of sun. Maybe getting a little color before her job interview. She seems so at home, so incredibly comfortable. Feels good. Then I notice that a few things have been re-arranged in my living room. A pink vase containing artificial silk flowers has been moved from the kitchen table to the living room. Her flowers, the celebrated vibrant medley mix, have taken their place, languishing in a glass jar that she's retrieved from where? I don't know. Maybe from one of the many cabinets in the kitchen, where I store stuff then forget about the stuff I've stored. She's obviously done an exploration since a blue ceramic plate from Mexico that I haven't seen since I moved in a couple of years ago is now a centerpiece on my carved wooden coffee table.

I poke my head out the door, say hello and ask if she'd like some breakfast, pitching my limited repertoire of avocado on toast and coffee. I'm also capable of scrambled eggs but can occasionally over or under do them so that may stretch my culinary skills and expose an inadequacy. Luckily, she goes for the avocado and toast with orange juice, and I return to the kitchen with an eye out for any other subtle changes in interior design. Sure enough, a set of Chinese brass candlesticks, formerly on my bookshelf, are now positioned in the middle of my kitchen table. It's all a bit spooky as I try to imagine her rummaging through my drawers and cabinets while I was blissfully taking a shower and thanking the gods that this angel had entered my life. I decide not to mention the shifts in décor. Maybe let her bring it up. No need to rock the boat. Especially when we are headed to Santa Barbara for her meeting with the organic farmers. Meaning that if she gets the job, she will move closer to me; I assume to her own place, unless she's already making my place, her place. Am I ready for that? I imagine the Tribal Elder's reaction, shaking his head, watery eyed, saying something profound about self-love, wholeness and spending time alone before reaching for his legal pad to jot down "The Seeker."

Suzanne eats, then dresses for her meeting; she looks great, casual in designer jeans and soft beige pullover but businesslike at the same time. I'd hire her in a heartbeat, maybe I already have. Not much traffic and it's a beautiful drive: the Pacific is a shimmering blue and the road flows like butter beneath my car. Radio's playing The Police and their 1983 song, "Every Breath You Take;" I feel like 1983, full of good times and rock 'n roll. I drop her off at the meeting site, a small restaurant on Main Street, agree to return in an hour and drive down to take in the beach. Thoughts of "this is it" dance like sugar plum fairies in my mind. A partner, someone to talk to, sleep with, make coffee for, drive to meetings, support .... Someone to re-arrange my house.

Suzanne says the meeting went well and they will let her know within the month; I'm thinking it's a done deal. She's smart, attractive, capable, who wouldn't hire her? I would, maybe I already have?

Back to the long and winding road leading to my long, straight and sometimes lonely driveway, and my son arrives for his weekend stay. He drives in, gets out of his car, walks through the front door and Suzanne is all over him. Hugs and kisses. Questions about his school, his interests, his girlfriends. I can't get a word in. It's all good, positive stuff but she's going overboard. He's an incredibly kind and sensitive young man and very polite but I can see him looking over at me as if to ask, who is this person, what's going on?

"Suzanne is visiting from New Mexico; she came for a job interview," I offer as if it's an excuse as she loosens her grip and allows him to sit down. It's then that I notice that the Kalim cushion that only yesterday decorated the white fabric of the sofa is no longer there. I look around the room and see it positioned beside my guitar near the hearth of the fireplace. That doesn't even make sense. Unless, I tell myself, that someone would choose to sit there as I perform. Red flags? The words cross my mind, but I don't want to see them. The Tribal Elder would call my response a denial. I deny the denial. Telling myself she's just nervous, like me, trying to make a good impression. She's beautiful. She's smart. She's sophisticated. She's sane. Please Dear God, let her be sane.

Another night, another bottle of wine, another avocado on toast, another slight shift in my furniture as my guitar is moved from its place beside the fireplace to the corner of the room and another ride to Santa Barbara and Suzanne, The Seeker, is gone, thirty-thousand feet in the air, looking down at the man she left behind. "Every step you take, I'll be watching you." Yes, I miss her already, it's true, even as I drive from the airport and head south on the 101.

Straight to the Elder.

*

This time the Elder, my friend and psychiatric mentor, after hearing of moved furniture, displaced guitars and overfamiliarity with my son, gives me a direct order regarding the new love in my life, something he rarely does.

"Run."

*

I follow his order, but not exactly in the direction in which it was given. A few weeks and a multitude of romantic phone calls later and I do run, courtesy of my air miles, straight to Taos. Greeted by a beautiful lady in a figure-hugging dress and a vintage Mercedes. Driven to a well-furnished guest house that Suzanne rents from a wealthy Taos family. She's taken time off from her job as produce manager at a branch of an organic food chain, and still hasn't heard from the farm in Santa Barbara; she's beginning to think it's not going to happen. I reassure her that the month isn't up but secretly have my doubts. She tells me she needs to get out of Taos. Needs to change jobs. Needs her own company and needs twenty-five-thousand dollars to start it up. I remain passive but feel the urge to come to her rescue. Become the rescuer. I'm still living on the capital I acquired from the split of money in the sale of the dream house; it's enough to keep me alive while I create another book, or another business, but sure as hell not enough to retire on. I am not rich, far from it. But I am a little crazy, although it doesn't feel that way at the time, and I could loan her the twenty-five if she really needed it. Another voice, which sounds like mine but a bit panicked, is screaming, "Don't do it!" at the top of its lungs, while somewhere in the background I hear an older, wiser voice calmly saying, "Run."

I hold my ground and stay quiet.

She begins to weep.

A half hour later and her tears have dried on my shoulder and night is falling. We dress, sip a glass of pre-dinner wine and head for the lights of town, which are fairly dim in a population of less than six thousand. Still, we find an atmospheric stucco-fronted restaurant with good, simple food and a guy playing Spanish love songs on a gut-stringed guitar. A bottle of wine later and I feel the stirrings of love. Back to the guest house, into bed, it's all so wonderful, and so … unreal. But it's real in the moment and the moment is all we've got: I turn off the lights.

Morning comes with a powdering of snow that soon turns into a full-scale blizzard, with the wind howling and visibility down to about ten feet beyond the bedroom window. Just enough to see Suzanne's old Mercedes with its iced windows and white blanketed roof; a small black bear is walking around it, he or she appears to be lost in the storm, maybe hoping for a lift to Southern California.

Bathroom conditions are tight, with hers being just off the single bedroom, within a few feet of the bed. Close enough that whoever is in the bed is privy to whatever sounds and conditions emanate from the adjacent room. I mention this because although bodily functions are normal, as in everyone uses the toilet, there's something about a new relationship that makes me want to deny they exist. Nothing like a loud burst of flatulence from a potential partner, reverberating in a porcelain bowl. Worse yet, an unpleasant scent wafting out from beneath the door. In other words, I'm concerned as to how I'm going to do what I have to do.

I get up, pull on my underwear and depart.

Suzanne has mercifully had the foresight to stock the small bathroom with matches, a box of incense and a floral scented spray, so I light a stick of musk, then use a technique taught to me by my mother, who, with her Victorian values, is probably the source of my current sound-smell phobia. I turn on the faucets, then the shower, creating a water cover-up as I cautiously relieve myself. Mission accomplished, I shave and use the shower, wrap up in a towel and return to the bed.

Suzanne awaits, and we spend another hour talking, cuddling and making love as the snow piles up beyond the paned-glass windows and the aroma of musk, mixed with floral air-freshener, floats in the air. It's all magic, like an old-time movie starring Ginger Rogers and Fred Astaire, something from the 1940s, romantic and innocent; or maybe we're an older version of Brad and Jennifer, or, more accurately, Brad and Angelina, as things will soon turn out. It's so quiet and comfortable, a long way from the despair of separation and divorce.

The subject of owning her own business resurfaces and I feel a chivalrous urge to offer money that I really don't have, but resist. Then she begins talking about her ex-husband, who she describes as an alcoholic hedge fund manager from New York. How he left her high and dry, with a minimum financial settlement, how he skillfully hid his assets while retaining custody of their single child. I keep wondering how an alcoholic could be so clever as to fool a judge. The child custody thing also puzzles me. As she speaks her entire demeanor changes. She's not beautiful anymore, not even pretty. She looks older and somehow vicious, as if thoughts and words can transform a human face. I feel I don't know this person and then I realize that I actually do not. She continues to rant as my cell phone begins to ring. I pick it up. My ex-wife's voice sounds like its coming from a different dimension.

"Richard?"

Suzanne's voice trails off and she becomes quiet as she focuses on me, sitting naked on the side of the bed, phone pressed to my ear.

"Richard?" my ex repeats. There's anxiety in her tone, something I'm not used to. She has always seemed so calm and collected.

"Yes?"

"I can hardly hear you … Where are you?"

"New Mexico."

She mentions my oldest son's name and I feel my stomach churn. Suddenly vulnerable, I pick the towel up from the floor and wrap it round me.

"He's being taken to emergency right now …"

When I left for this trip he was at college, in bed with what he said was the worst stomachache he'd ever had. His mother and I blamed it on food poisoning.

"They think his appendix burst."

I know that can be fatal. I feel powerless. "I'll get there as fast as I can."

I hear what sounds like an audible groan from Suzanne.

"I'm headed up north to be with him right now," my ex says. "I'll call and let you know how he is."

The feelings are overwhelming. The fear and uncertainty. Visualizing our child lying on a gurney, headed to surgery. Or worse. Suddenly I feel close to my ex, as only two people who share the bond of a child or children can feel.

"I'll get home as quick as I can," I promise. "Goodbye."

I turn to the stranger beside me.

"You're still in love with her, aren't you?" she says; her voice an accusation.

My mind is a roller-coaster, but one thought is recurring: how do I get out of here?

"Your ex-wife. You still love her, don't you?"

Maybe I do. Maybe I don't, but, at this moment, I sure as hell don't love the angry lady beside me.

"You feel like you're trapped here with me."

I look out the window. Snow is still coming down, but it's no longer a blizzard. I'm wondering when I can get a flight, and there's room for nothing here, but honesty.

"Yes, I do," I answer.

"What about me?" Suzanne continues. "You said we'd be together. We'd have a business together. Dinner parties. Trips to Europe. You lied. I'm so fed up with men who lie. You liar."

Now I'm getting angry.

"My son's in the emergency room with a burst appendix."

She continues to glare. Her eyes look dark, beady, and very close together. Aimed at me, like a double-barreled shotgun; I don't think she even knows what a burst appendix is, or the severity of it.

"You said we'd be together when you were ninety," she continues. "Now you're running away."

I cannot remember saying any of these things, particularly the part about being together at ninety. In fact, I'm sure I didn't say that.

"Liar," she repeats, adding a touch of vitriol.

"I really need to go home," I say flatly. "When do you think the airport will open?"

"Why did you even come here, why?"

She's crying and I feel terrible, not just for my son in the emergency room, but for the beautiful woman lying naked in front of me who has become suddenly ugly from bitterness and disappointment. And I do feel like a prisoner. Locked in this room and locked-up inside. Confused. A thousand miles from anywhere. Powerless to help anyone.

The snow subsides, then stops. I phone the airport and am told they'll be open in the morning. I book a flight for 10 AM. Suzanne and I are not speaking. Not so much out of animosity but because we really have nothing to say. My ex-wife phones again. My son will be okay. The appendix did burst but they have him on strong antibiotics to prevent the spread of infection. The doctors have assured her that our boy will be all right. Relief settles over me as dusk settles upon the stark white outside the windows, finally giving way to a full moon that casts a golden glow. Beauty all around, if I could just see through this chaos in my mind.

"I'm sorry," I say to Suzanne. "Really sorry."

She meets my eyes and raises her hands, as if to say, "What are we going to do now?"

"Will you take me to the airport in the morning?" I ask.

"Yes."

Morning comes and our brief romance is over. I know it; she knows it. We were both exposed and neither liked what they saw. We stop for breakfast on the way to the airport. Coffee, toast, an omelet, a bowl of oatmeal, two people who are not exactly sure of what happened and what happens next. Two strangers who, for a moment, thought they were not. This time I don't feel like I'm escaping, fleeing through the gates of the English Rose mansion to an online life of freedom and adventure. I know I'm headed back to that lonely place.

Suzanne is stuck on one thing. "You still love your ex-wife," she insists. "I could tell when you were talking on the phone. You love her."

I don't want to argue.

"She's the mother of my children," I answer, and leave it at that, but one thing I do know, one thing this trip has taught me; it's going to take a long time to get close to someone new. To trust someone. To trust myself.

"You need to get over her," she continues, with a little edge to her voice. "You can't expect to have a new relationship if you haven't left the old one behind. It's not fair."

"No, it's not." I agree.

"I know I overstepped my boundaries yesterday," she continues, softening.

"It's okay. It really is."

Out the door, into her car and to the airport. Things have eased between us and knowing that my son will be okay has relaxed me. She walks with me towards the departure lounge. The flight is called.

"Will I ever see you again?" she asks.

The question catches me flat-footed. I already know the answer, or I think I know the answer, but I don't say it. I understand why she's asking. It's all about that search for a connection; someone to walk with and hold onto in the night. None of us want to go back to looking at faces on the computer screen, trying to read behind the eyes, see behind the mask. Reading profiles. Searching for a kindred soul.

And me, I need some time on my own. To heal. There, I've said it, to myself. The same thing the Elder says, the same thing I know inside but have not wanted to admit. Stare into the abyss.

"I'll phone you," I say. A hug, A light kiss and I walk away.

The next two hours, in the air, I spend with my sons, those beautiful young men with everything in front of them. Praying for their health and happiness yet knowing that no one here gets out alive; and we all learn our lessons along the way.

Three days pass. My oldest son is out of trouble. Laughing on the phone. Getting ready to leave the hospital. Coming home for a few days. He may not even need to have the perforated organ removed. Everything has become less invasive these days, at least with medicine. In matters of the heart, nothing has changed, except the internet.

I phone Suzanne as I promised I would, but the tone of our conversation has changed. We both know what we knew that day at the airport. Neither is ready for a relationship, at least not this relationship. She needs something that I am unable to give, and I need something that I'm not even sure exists, at least not from another person. We hang up as friends, but friends who are unlikely to speak again, because the friendship was founded on need and fantasy.

I swear off online dating, suspending my membership. Determined to spend time alone. Visit the Tribal Elder. Sit. Talk. Then, towards the close of our time together, he pops the million-dollar question, maybe even more than a million, now that the divorce has been settled.

"Are you still in love with your ex-wife?"

This time I'm ready.

"No," I answer.

The Elder smiles.

"Good. That's the first step towards healing." Then, carefully, he writes the name Suzanne on his pad, beneath Michelle and English Rose. The list is growing.

*

Think. Meditate. Try to establish a connection with myself, an understanding, a compassion.

But the temptation is always there; go online, take a look around; you know she's out there, like a red kite, dancing high in the sky, shaped like a heart.

The dating site continues to bombard me with "likes" and "messages" that I can only see if I re-activate my membership. It's just business, providing a service that feeds off the basic need for social and intimate companionship. Offering a form of salvation, but how many of us are truly ready to be saved? How many at our age can actually lay down the baggage we have accumulated over the years? How many are actually available, physically, spiritually, and emotionally?

How many have done the inner work required for a sustainable relationship?

I travel my new path to self-love for a little over a week. Withdrawal symptoms include severe bouts of hopelessness while staring down the rock-walled driveway to oblivion, going over all past marriages, love affairs and connections in ruthless detail and blaming myself for much of my pain. Beginning three books. Deleting them all. Choices are everywhere. And then, one gray wet morning, after a restless night, I can't take it anymore. Sitting down at the computer, I google the site and re-activate my membership, then up the ante by subscribing to two other online dating sites. I feel a certain guilt, a certain weakness, a definite betrayal of the Tribal Elder and his wisdom, and a betrayal of my own self-discipline … plus lots of excitement.

I am an addict.

***

~8~

Several online dates follow. Smarter now, maybe wiser, following my lawyer's advice regarding the cost of dinners and a long evening with someone who has no real interest in me, or me in her; if I don't feel a connection from the initial messages and photos and am just wanting to take a look, a "just in case" kind of thing, I confine my occasional dates to coffee bars or maybe a rendezvous at the beach, basking in the negative ions and the sound of the surf. If upon meeting there is nothing much in the form of connection, at least I can ask questions and make friends, though for the most part these are not lasting friendships. "Do you get lonely?" is one of my favorite questions, because I am genuinely interested to learn if others feel as I do. Makes me feel less isolated knowing that these feelings are universal, or maybe to understand that if I give these emotions and myself more time, as the Elder has suggested, I, too, will be happy on my own, complete in a way that I am not now and, perhaps, have never been. More often than not the women's answer is something like, "Yes, sometimes I get lonely but not often," or "No, I'm good on my own," and many times I hear, "I love being on my own." These answers are from my dates. When I ask the same question to my male counterparts the answers weigh heavily in the "Yes, I'm lonely a lot" group, particularly those without immediate family; or, like me, with a coast-to-coast distance between myself and my only blood relative, my brother. It's fun on the telephone but there's nothing like sharing the company of someone close, someone who knows who you are and with whom you have a history. My sons are both in college and it's their turn to grow and explore. Good to know they are well and healthy, but I don't want to lean on them, nor do I actually have any need to. I want them to develop their own independence. I'm looking for a new female connection, not a retreat to the known.

Over time, and with lot of questions and conversation, I understand that women, at least those I've talked to about it, do better alone than men. Seems they form faster and more lasting social connections, women's groups, one-on-one friendships; they've got yoga, dancing, full-moon circles and various women empowerment groups. They also generally outlive men, so maybe its genetic. Truth is, there are more lonely men than women.

The other fact that I learn after another year into my online explorations is that as many dates as I have and even when I like the person sitting across from me at the restaurant or coffee bar, a feeling has developed that the next woman might be better: more compatible, more beautiful, brighter, more sophisticated, more in tune with me, a better connection, or the new love of my life. I do not want to settle. I'm lonely, but I am less and less desperate. Meeting new women online has become like a trip to the candy store, wanting to taste everything that looks good; and that is at the heart of the online addiction: there is always one more. It's the same for many of my dates; I'm not the only male on their agenda.

There are millions of us out there and surely, if we keep trying, we will find the perfect partner, the diamond in the sand.

And then ... some prefer the freedom of a single life, the freedom to travel, to look around, sample whatever's available and maybe never be monogamous again; or, in some cases, never need another full-time companion, in many cases adopting the attitude that , "sex is so over-rated." Well... I'm not there yet.

In total, counting both marriages, I was partnered for thirty-six years, so I am used to the companionship, the feeling of another presence in the house; having someone to talk to, share a bed, intimacy. That's the good part, but the fact is, over half of marriages end in divorce. The alternative is the bad marriage or a bad relationship, kept alive for the sake of finances or the fear of going it alone, and these arrangements often include separate bedrooms, feelings of isolation, loneliness, animosity, quarrelling and the claustrophobic sensation of being trapped. I lived like that for a while, and have several friends living like that now. Preferring company of any sort to an empty house and all the feelings that go with it. Self-discovery can be a rough voyage.

*

My online romantic life slows down; I've now been making the cyber-rounds for nearly two years, long enough that I'm not the new kid on the block, far from it; more like the old man on the site. Although I'm still only sixty-one… At least, online.

The Tribal Elder declares me on the mend. Notations on his legal pad have also slowed, and it's been a while since he added a new name to the list.

Still, I reach out with my own "likes" and messages, but many of my messages are not returned, and most don't make it to the phone call stage. My friend Oatmeal Jane suggests I may be being too aggressive with my messaging. Suggesting an exchange of phone numbers should not take place before the third or fourth communication, certainly not on the first or second. But … I've been sent requests for my number on the first message, why should it be any different for a man? Because, she explains, men can be seen as predatory while women are not. It's a case of online etiquette, learn or suffer.

*

It has been a dry two months, very dry, with hardly any messages sent to me from the main site and only a few returns from the ones I've sent out. I'm concerned but not in total despair. Assuring myself that there is a divine plan and just the right person is out there and will eventually appear.

The Tribal Elder is reassuring. "This is very healthy, exactly what you need," he says.

"What is that?"

"More time alone. More honesty with yourself."

My honest self considers the reality that I may live alone for the rest of my life. My grandfather, having lost his wife when he was only a few years older than I am, continued alone for another twenty years. I recall visiting him, seated in a warmly upholstered parlor chair in his small living room, watching Lawrence Welk, bandleader and accordionist, make his "champagne music" on the TV. Between anthems, I asked, "Do you ever get lonely?"

"Of course, I do," he replied. "But I live with it." Silencing me with his hand as Lawrence waved his baton, counted "a one an' a two an' a three" and the bubble machine floated streams of pink soap, water and air across the television screen as the big band launched into another standard.

Aside from Lawrence Welk, living with loneliness meant regular dinners at the Pomfret Club, and the occasional company of a few close friends, including a skeletally thin retired school teacher, a South African woman of undetermined age who appeared ancient to me, like some Egyptian mummy, declared herself a maiden lady, which I assumed meant she was still a virgin at seventy-seven, and called him at five o'clock every evening. I am uncertain as to the nature of their conversations but more often than not, Grandpa would say a few words, then slam the phone down, look at me, shake his head and declare, "She's crazy. That woman is crazy." Crazy enough that he preferred the alternative, his own cooking, which was easily as bad as mine, his own bedroom and, for the most part, his own company.

I am not quite ready to walk my grandfather's path. Besides, he did not have the option of online dating, so those five o'clock phone calls were his main shot at a companion. I've got thousands of options. Thousands of potential companions. But ... finding the right one, the magical other, that's the challenge.

*

I switch my attention to another dating site, known for quick hook-ups and favored by a younger crowd, looking more for a one-night stand than the next long-termer, where a single swipe of the hand against a cell phone decides the fate of the face on the screen. "Not for me" and I swipe to the left; "Oh, yes, I like her" and I swipe to the right, like a dance with the fingers. The positive right swipe sends a message to the chosen party and then it's up to her to respond. I've watched my oldest son do this, and he seems to be inundated with gorgeous young babes. Maybe dad can get in on the act.

I will also admit there were times, when I still felt that there was life ahead and juice below, that the idea of sex with a stranger was enough to get me online. Something without attachment, something to get me through the night, straighten my mind and lead me back to the true and nearly holy quest for the real thing, and maybe, just maybe that single swipe would lead me to the magical other. You never know, online.

*

It's nine o'clock in the evening, I've had two glasses of red wine, the fire is turning to ember, and it's nearly bedtime for the man in search of himself but hoping for an intermediary who will offer unadulterated eroticism and then vanish like the after-scent of a sweet perfume. I've got my cell phone in hand and I'm swiping madly. Mostly to the left; in fact, everything is going left. In fact, I'm going left so fast that I'm afraid I might miss a potential right swipe. It's a cellular Rolodex, and my age group, fifty-five to seventy, is looking fairly decrepit, many in need of dental repair, a gym membership or a new hair stylist. Swipe. Swipe, swipe and then ...

Her face is unusual, not particularly feminine, and not pretty or beautiful by the common definition of the word but striking. Angular and proud, there is an aristocratic air about her features; maybe it's her expression: nonchalant, detached, with piercing blue eyes, a wide mouth with full sensuous lips. Her eyebrows appear to be painted on, which I definitely don't like, but her long blonde hair is luxurious and flowing. I stop. Inhale. Sip the last of the wine. Scroll down to see more photos She's dressed in an evening gown. Stunning. Coming out of the water on a tropical beach. Her body looks well-made and strong, with well-shaped and well-muscled legs, wide sculpted shoulders. In a land of cart horses, I've stumbled upon a thoroughbred. Read on. Originally from Denmark, her name is given as Grace, as in Amazing, her age as fifty-nine, as in hopefully she's telling the truth, and her height is six-feet-one, as in I'm in trouble. I stop again. Put the glass down on the table. I am five-feet-nine, on a good day. What would a woman of six-feet-one think of dating a man four or five inches shorter than she? What would we look like going into a restaurant, with my head resting on her shoulder? Or ballroom dancing, that could be a major problem, not that I do any of it, and how about a trip down the aisle, not that I intend to, but you never know. And what about high heels? Rationalize quickly. There are many Hollywood celebrities who have large height differences between themselves and their female companions, starting with the five-foot-two-inch survivor of the silent film era, Mickey Rooney, who, born in 1920, was married eight times and involved with women as high as six-feet-two; a talented man who never let height get in the way of his love life. Then there's Tom Cruise and Danny DeVito, who tips the scales at four-ten, and Al Pacino and many more in the five-nine and under category. No, I can't let height become a factor. Besides, if Grace has a problem with it, she won't message me back, since once I swipe right the decision to make contact is all up to her. But where does she live? I look down at her description and see, Ventura. I can't believe it. She's virtually on my doorstep, eleven miles west, with a sea view. Occupation? Personal trainer, which would explain her well-developed body and be a great starting point for conversation since I've been involved with exercise and coaching people for many years, a sideline to my writing. Grace is just too impressive all around for a snide left swipe.

I commit. Swiping to the right as if I'm throwing a Hail Mary pass at the Superbowl.

There, I've done it. The ball's in the air. I'll buy shoe lifts if necessary.

Then, the usual wait begins. What will she think of my profile? My photos? My height? How many days will I wait to hear back? Will I ever hear back?

About to unfold from the sofa and climb the tiled stairs to my bedroom and pop a few Melatonin when my phone pings. I look down. It's a message from Grace. Wow, from swipe right to a reply in under three minutes; this breaks my old online record by a full day. I breathe out slowly, steadying myself and hoping for the best. No matter how many times I go through this I'm always a shade nervous of a polite rejection.

"Richard. Love your profile. Love your photo. Love that you appreciate me. Hope you like tall girls."

Oh, I do, Grace, I do.

Contemplate another glass of wine and several clever replies involving Mickey Rooney but choose discipline instead. Sometimes wine causes me to exercise my hybrid sense of humor, which, mainly acquired in London, involves saying or writing things with a straight face or steady hand that make absolutely no sense to the recipient and are sometimes deemed offensive. Got to use some control here; I answer with an innocuous, "If you don't mind 5-9, I love 6-1."

I've barely hit send when she responds, "What are you doing tonight?"

It's 8:45 and the truth is, I'm headed up to bed.

I reply, "Not much. Sitting here having a glass of wine, looking at pictures of you."

"Want to come over?"

At first, I am taken aback. I have always been sensitive to being too aggressive and fast off the mark, but Grace is quicker. I study her words as if looking for a deeper message. "Want to come over?" Simple as that. Well, do you, or don't you? Do you feel lucky, punk? But I hate driving at night; the glare from oncoming cars blinds me. What if I crash? What if I miss the opportunity to meet a fantastic woman? I go back to her picture. She looks strong and assertive, not the kind to trifle with indecision. A surge of adrenaline kicks in and I am no longer ready for bed, not tired at all, in fact if my knees could manage anything beyond a fast-paced walk, I'd sprint to Ventura. Okay, this may not be the love of my life, the answer to my lonely prayers, or the cure for my melancholia, but then again it could be. Or, it could be just the erotic adventure I need, and I'll never know if I don't take a chance.

"You've just made my evening." I answer. "What is your address?"

She sends me an address for a place just off The Avenue, which used to be the rough northern edge of Ventura and has been the home to the Hells Angels clubhouse for many years but has recently seen a resurgence in art studios and shops and has a growing bohemian atmosphere.

She follows with a phone number and I'm up the stairs, into the shower, shaved, sprinkled with cologne, dressed, including my new Calvin Klein black boxers with the buttoned fly, grab a bottle of red wine, and out the door. Not much glare on my drive out of town. No collisions, and the eleven miles goes seamlessly, as my navigation guides me off the highway at the Main Street exit, down past two traffic lights and left to what appears to be a converted warehouse at the western end of the Avenue. Lots of big, old buildings and few streetlights. Paranoia creeps in. Could this be a set-up? Luring a lonely cyberspace traveler to a dark, secluded destination? Held for ransom? Molested? Is English Rose behind the scenes, with my bottle of Clicquot in her hand, about to claim her revenge for my escape from Alcatraz?

My nav tells me I have arrived. Park on the street, turn off the car and look around. It's 9:45 and there is still some pedestrian traffic; the people I see all look relatively civilized, walking hand in hand, carrying bags, or riding bikes along the sidewalk. I get out of my car, lock up, and walk to the nearest building, then check Grace's address against the ones given on a large mounted board out front. Sure enough, there it is. I wander around a bit till I find the door, which is on the street level of the building and to the side. Stand there for a moment. Is this what I want to be doing? There's something that feels slightly sleezy about the whole thing, and that something could be me, but … here I am, with no place to go but home, or in. I ring the entry bell and wait, with the feeling that I am in the wrong place at the wrong time, doing the wrong thing. Almost turn to leave when the door opens.

"You made it," she says.

I feel dwarfed but fascinated. Grace is big and seems to fill the entire frame of the door, but very proportionate and actually beautiful in an Icelandic, Viking kind of way. Her beauty is cold as opposed to the warm dark looks of a South American. She's a stunning iceberg. And here I am, the five-foot-nine Titanic.

"Please, come in," she says. She's also got the hint of an accent which reminds me that Denmark was included in her profile.

I enter a small apartment with a wrap-around sofa, lit by a dim table lamp and several candles, and featuring dozens of shoes strewn about or stacked against the walls: high heels, low heels, no heels, sandals and boots, in rainbow shades of blues and golds. I don't quite know what to say, other than, "Wow, you're really into shoes."

Grace laughs, leads me to the sofa, takes the bottle of wine from my hand, walks to the kitchen area of the room and uncorks it. Bringing me back a full crystal glass. She sits down beside me and touches her glass to mine. Clink. Hopefully, the wine will relax me, because I just don't feel right. It's a strange feeling, an energy that seems out of alignment. Without a lot of conversation, I lower my head and stare at my feet; I'm wearing flip-flops and suddenly my toenails look untrimmed and I'm hoping Grace doesn't notice. Then, I look at her feet, which are bare and large, with pale pink nail varnish. Considerably larger than my own, but then, I don't have big feet, size nine and a half, which according to my estimates would make Grace's somewhere around size eleven, maybe twelve, maybe not so unusual for such a big girl. I glance again at the many pairs of shoes that decorate the space; they all look very large. Maybe she has a foot fetish; I certainly seem to as I continue staring at my own feet, then hers, comparing toe length and curvatures. Feet are so distinct. Her big toe fans out at the tip, while my second toe, right foot, has become hammered by being crunched in cowboy boots. All in all, I'm not a fan of feet but can't stop looking at them.

Conversation is minimal. I ask her where she does her personal training. Generally, at the client's residence, she explains, using bodyweight exercises that she learned when she practiced gymnastics and resistance bands. She's only been doing it for a short time; before that she was a beautician but got fed up with rude clients and long hours. I look down at her hands, long strong fingers, the backs are roped with veins. Easier to think of those hands lifting a forty-five-pound dumbbell than applying eyeliner. She looks at me and smiles. Something is starting to gel, explaining the uneasy feeling I've had since I entered her apartment.

"Do you want a little more wine?" As she speaks, I am suddenly aware of the depth of her voice, like its coming right up from her belly, or even lower.

"Sure," I answer, trying to figure out what to do.

As she bends to take my glass, I see the beginnings of a bald patch on the top of her head. The condition is called male pattern baldness, and it is now obvious, or I think it is: Grace is a man, which explains the feelings I've had since entering her place. I'm not angry. In fact, I am a little frightened. What does she want from me and how do I get out of here? She gets up to fill my glass and I watch her from behind; even in her black baggy harem pants she looks sturdy and moves well, and the arms coming from her loose beige knit top look strong. I could bolt for the door but that doesn't feel right, she's not my enemy; besides, she might tackle me. But where is this all going? I recall my brief wrestling match with English Rose and envision a real tussle with Grace. One that I may lose, but I've got to do something.

The wine arrives and she sits down, this time a little closer. What if I ask if she's a man, and she turns out to be female? What do I say then? "Sorry, but I noticed you are going bald and just had to ask." No, that's too indelicate. I meet her eyes then look down casually, checking for an Adam's apple. Yep, there it is. My imagination ploughs on. Does this woman have a penis? And, if she does, what does she intend to do with it? I put an end to the paranoia with a single statement.

"It's probably time for me to go."

She looks at me; it's a strange look, not angry, not sad, just curious. Like she knows what I'm thinking.

"How carefully did you read my profile?" she asks.

"Really just glanced at it," I reply.

"So, you didn't know I was transsexual when you got here?"

"No idea," I confess.

She smiles, "You must be shocked."

"A little," I say, beginning to relax for the first time in an hour.

"Well … I actually didn't write transsexual, I only wrote trans, so you're forgiven for missing it."

"Have you ever had this happen before?" I ask.

"You're the first guy to respond," she says.

Now I feel guilty. Like she's trusted me and I've let her down.

"Drink the wine. Don't worry, I'm not going to rape you," she adds with a touch of sarcasm. "Even though you're kind of cute, in an older sort of way."

I laugh. She laughs, and we actually start talking. About her childhood in Copenhagen, then moving to Kansas at twelve years old, with the agonies of not knowing why she felt the way she felt about her gender. Always identifying herself as a girl. The ridicule. The absolute isolation. The loneliness. Her attempted suicide at seventeen. Leaving Wichita to move to Hollywood, where she thought she would be accepted. And always that feeling, that overwhelming feeling, that she was stuck in the wrong body. Saving her money for surgery, a sex reassignment. Intending to have it done in Thailand, where it costs less than half of what it does in the United States.

By the time Grace has finished, I've laughed, and I've cried, and if I had the money in my pocket for her surgery, I'd give it to her. She is honest, and more than that, she is courageous.

It's one o'clock by the time I roll up the driveway to my house. I don't feel so lonely tonight. Not so isolated. Maybe a little humbler and a little less indulgent. There are a lot of people out there, and everyone has their story. I'm just one of them.

Goodnight, Grace. Bless your heart and bless your twenty-eight pairs of shoes.

***

~9~

Not so many swipes, not so many messages, more time alone. I am beginning, just beginning, to realize something: there is no one out there who can rescue me, and the only authentic and worthwhile love is that love that allows the other to be what and who they are. I get this, and I am able to practice it on a short-term basis, as in with close friends, but can I actually live it inside a love relationship?

I need to stand on my own, with no one to prop me up, either emotionally or financially. And, the truth is, I've never done it. For thirty-six years I've had a partner to lean on, to share my rants and my rages, my triumphs and disappointments, to share love, to share doubt and suffering, not to mention the rent. To care for me in one way or another. How many of us are aware of this? Yet, without the ability to stand on one's own, to be individuated, there is no chance of finding the *magical other*, to form a lasting relationship, not a healthy one anyway; codependence requires that one person will be consumed by the other, or a joint consumption, like a mutual stranglehold, with no way out but suffocation.

Sounds strange, coming from a seventy-year-old man, but our life's lessons come, at times, when they are least expected, and, perhaps, just when they are supposed to.

I agree; it's takes at least a year, maybe two, to really know another person, enough time for the echoes of past traumas to manifest; traumas that are often suffered before the age of seven, before the young mind can distinguish between darkness and light, good or evil. Absorbing the horror and pain, forcing it down into the basement of the subconscious. When summoned, the shadows that inhabit this ominous place emerge, marching up the stairs, pounding on the door to the living room. Demanding entry. Then … it takes only the right, or wrong word or situation to trigger a full manifestation; and the door comes crashing down and the monster looms.

Face to face, the partner is stunned, in shock.

"It's me," the monster growls. "And I'm gonna' destroy everything you've got."

Enter the Tribal Elder … "Run!"

*

I'm making progress on the road to independence, but not enough to stop checking the dating sites at least twice a day. Feeling that I've spent enough time in the monastery; I need to get out in the real world again. Test the waters.

And here it comes, not quite the real world but the only world that has a non-stop kaleidoscope of everything I'm looking for, or everything I think I'm looking for.

I scroll through my "searches" on the site and hit upon someone new; someone who was not there yesterday. I scroll down, check a couple more faces, then return. There's just something about this one. Strange how it works. Even though it's only an image, there is still that law of attraction. Maybe it's the eyes, a smile, a curl in the hair, the way she is dressed, even a necklace, an energy that radiates, but there's always something that connects. This one is in the eyes, big, brown and soulful.

Or maybe it's because her location is given as Santa Barbara, forty-five minutes away, which sure beats a trip to Taos.

Her screen name is Clair de Lune. I know that's a famous poem or song, but I google it anyway, maybe the web will supply something clever and intelligent to say if I choose to send a message. Clair de Lune, light of the moon, based on an 18th century poem by Paul Verlaine, portraying the human soul as beautiful and full of music, but in a minor key. I play the guitar, and I prefer the minor chords. I understand beauty, particularly when its tinged with sadness.

Studying her profile pictures inspires a different melody; it's a 20th century song by Van Morrison that talks about thumping hearts, misty mornings and a brown-eyed girl.

Hello Clair de Lune, with your soulful brown eyes and shy smile. Hello my brown-eyed girl. Here I come. Seventy years young; oh, how I hate that term "young," why don't we just say, seventy-years-old and ready to rock … if my knee doesn't buckle.

Not so fast.

Have I learned anything?

Read her profile carefully, scan for words like "trans" or "polyamorous" or anything beyond my accepted norms of sexuality. Nothing. Her profile says she is fifty-four years old, which makes her sixteen years younger than me in real time, but in cyberspace I've just turned sixty-two, so the cyber-gap is only eight. Besides, in real time, Clair may be sixty. Who knows how old her pictures are? Does anyone tell the truth, or post current photos? Onwards. Height: five-feet-six. Great, no need for lifts. Occupation: Pilates instructor, formerly a schoolteacher, a dancer; she sings and plays the guitar, and is looking for a man aged fifty-three to sixty-five. I'm still in the game, because I've cheated my way to the table. Bluffing. I have a moment of guilt. Is it time to own up about my age? No, not yet. Maybe next time, or I'll do what so many of my friends do, I'll reveal my geriatric status during our first date, over the age-defying glow of a candlelit dinner, immersed in the fountain of youth poured from a bottle of wine. Head held high to tighten my neck. Smiling beatifically. Relying on sheer charm and animal magnetism to win Clair de Lune's heart. Yes, that will work, along with an ascot tie and a Jack Sparrow smile. Why is age such a big deal? And … is Clair de Lune even going to respond to my message? She's new on the site, so she'll be inundated. Somehow, I've got to come up with something original, authentic.

Have I learned anything else?

Maybe to accept and put up with this ache that so often resides inside me. This feeling that something is missing, that something is unfulfilled, been left undone; it is a longing, a constant yearning. It is that ache that makes me want to pick up the telephone and seek rescue: call my brother, or a friend, invite someone to dinner, go online and reach out to another stranger, try and soothe the pain; yet the wiser, more knowing part of me, understands that the ache is also a teacher, like pain and suffering but without the sharp edges. If pain is a scalpel, the ache is a blunt force instrument, its work is accomplished through a continual pressure.

At times, the ache vanishes, and I am left in the here and now, in the present tense, happy to be who I am and where I am, without the drain of anxiety and fear. I'd like to spend more time in the present, which is exactly why exercise, breathing and meditation is so important. These disciplines, done correctly, encourage a body awareness that cuts through the negativity and grounds one in the moment.

I'm getting there, or here, more often, but something is still missing.

*

"Hello Clair, I've read your profile and see you are a Pilates instructor. Pilates has always been an interest of mine. I practiced in London at the studio of an ex-dancer who was a student of Joe Pilates' wife, Clara. I worked with him for over a year, and I now teach classes in breath and movement, trying to incorporate the basic Pilates principles into my classes. Pilates made me aware of the pelvic floor, so I owe Joe for that one. Where, in Santa Barbara do you teach?"

I re-read my message several times. It certainly lacks my usual sardonic humor, but sometimes that humor sinks me. I cannot think of anything else to write, other than the usual "love your pictures," or "really like you profile" kind of thing. I figure that this allows for a response without a commitment; too early to ask for a phone number or suggest a cup of coffee. Patience, I'm learning by necessity.

Clair's response arrives a day later. Pleasant enough, she says, "Hello, your profile sounds interesting. Great that you practiced Pilates. Are your photographs recent?" Well ... some of them are. Then she goes on to give me the name of a studio just off State Street in Santa Barbara. Her message is signed, Angelina.

She's asked about my photos, which means she's interested. That's a big hurdle, since many women on the receiving end of various messages never respond; and why would they, when I've heard from several that men, even at my age, have been known to send photos of body parts, including hairy chests and wrinkled arms, sagging butts, and, if the recipient is particularly unlucky, a full-on genital shot, a sure-fire aphrodisiac.

An idea comes to me. It's risky but exciting at the same time. I won't answer her message, not online, anyway. Instead, I google the name of the Pilates studio she's given me, get a phone number and, without second thoughts, dial the number. Nervous, I feel like a kid on the cusp of getting caught at something he shouldn't be doing. Maybe I've been alone for too long and lost the plot, but I believe my idea has originality and there's something fun about it, like a movie, a romantic comedy.

A female voice answers: I ask if Angelina is available. Hoping it's not her on the phone, because, if it is, I'm sure as hell not going to identify myself. Told she won't be in till tomorrow at ten. At this point I take a leap of faith and book an appointment for a private lesson with Angelina, at three o'clock tomorrow afternoon, her first availability. Leave my name and telephone number and put down the phone. My heart is beating fast; I've done it.

Visions of being removed in handcuffs from the Pilates studio, or wrenched from my supine position on the Reformer and tossed out the door by a couple of well-muscled pelvic floors, crumpled into a fetal position on the sidewalk while the divine Angelina points her finger at me and shouts, "Yes that's him, the internet stalker!"

Okay, I don't have to go to the appointment. I only gave my name as Richard, no last name; there are lots of Richards in the world, even a few "Dicks," of which I am now officially one, and if I don't look enough like my photograph, she won't recognize me anyway; I can slip in quietly, take the lesson, pay and leave.

Dear God, what have I done?

Okay, calm down, you don't need to decide till tomorrow at 2 o'clock, I tell myself. You can cancel the lesson or be a "no-show" and simply respond to her message in the normal fashion. No need to panic. Nothing lost, not yet.

***

~10~

Santa Barbara is a city of about one hundred thousand people located on the central California coast. The pink and gold peaks of the Santa Ynez mountains form the backdrop while the white beaches and the shimmering Pacific Ocean wait with open arms at the western end of State Street, the main artery through town. The buildings are mostly Mediterranean in style, with their red tiled roofs giving the place an old Spanish feel. It's a feel I associate with Southern California and one of the main reasons I moved here from the East Coast. Reminiscent of the South of France, or the South of Spain, sunny and warm, with theatres and outdoor cafés and music in the streets, except everyone speaks English. There is also a vast population of homeless people, who provide a stark contrast to the affluent shops and chic restaurants with their five-hundred and fifty dollars per person menus.

According to my dashboard thermometer it's a perfect seventy-two degrees when I take a right on State Street and follow my navigation up the palm-lined avenue to Carrillo, then swing another right at a sign that indicates a public parking lot. Everything looks dream-like through the dark tint windows of my Volt, and I'm actually looking forward to my Pilates class. Dream-like, including the cop on his big Honda with his flashers on. I pull over to let him by, but he doesn't go by; then I pull into the lot, go up a ramp to the first floor and he's right behind me.

It's two-forty-five when I turn off the engine, and the police officer has already dismounted and is standing beside my window. He's Asian, and appears to be a cop in miniature, not more than five-two and thin as a spoke. But what he lacks in stature he makes up for in attitude. He's fuming; like I can feel the heat coming off the silver-mirrored lenses of his Ray-Bans.

Power down my window.

"Yes, sir?"

"Driver's license and registration please."

Keep it low-key and respectful. "May I ask you what the problem is?" I venture, as I produce my wallet and locate my driver's license. The insurance papers are buried somewhere in the console and it takes a minute or so of fumbling to find them. Hand them over and he walks back to his bike to call me in. I've still got no idea what this is all about.

Meanwhile, time's running out. The Reformer is waiting. Clair de Lune is calling, and I've got five minutes to get to the Pilates studio on time.

Mini cop returns. Hands me back my papers.

"Why didn't you pull over when I signaled you on State Street?"

"I honestly didn't see you," I answer. "And when I did, just before I turned in to this lot, I had no idea you were following me."

He nods his head. Looking skeptical.

"The tint on your front windows is illegal," he goes on.

I have no idea what he means.

"Illegal?"

"Too dark."

"But that's the way the car was sold to me," I say.

"Was it pre-owned?"

"Yes," I answer. Recalling the fast-talking dealer in Orange County with his lot full of Ford pick-ups, Chevy Corvettes and Dodge Chargers. The black Volt stood out like a gentleman amongst thugs. Eight thousand miles on the clock, with a plug-in electric engine, low profile and tinted windows, giving it just that hint of the street, sort of an environmentalist gangster's ride.

"The vehicle might have come in from out of state." he says, sounding like Sherlock Holmes on the verge of cracking a case, "these windows are not safe at night and I couldn't identify you through the glass. You're not legal, not in California."

With that he looks up, allowing me a less than reassuring glimpse of my distorted reflection in his silver shades as he hands me the fix-it ticket.

"You've got thirty days," he concludes, pivoting sharply to walk back to his motorcycle. He reminds me of RoboCop, or the Terminator, but smaller, much smaller.

I'm now ten minutes late and I don't feel good about the tint, the time, about anything. Luckily, I spot the wooden sign above the plate glass on the other side of the road and hustle over. It's a fair-sized place and I can see all of the familiar machines through the window, their skeletal framework adorned with springs, bars, a trapeze and padded cushions, with two instructors guiding their pupils through movements I haven't performed in thirty years.

My eyes search for Clair de Lune. I don't see her.

Walk in, to the front desk, announce myself to a silver-haired lady, older, but probably younger than me, and apologize that I'm late. She smiles, assures me that it's okay, picks up a phone and hits an intercom button.

"Your three-o'clock is here," she says.

Seconds later Clair de Lune appears from a room at the back of the studio. She is identical to her photos, as if they were taken an hour ago. Wearing a simple white tank top and gray yoga pants that stop mid-way down her calves. Her feet are bare, and definitely not size twelve.

If she recognizes me, she doesn't show it. Walking forward with an outstretched hand.

"Hello, Richard."

Does she know who I am, or doesn't she? At least she didn't call me Dick.

"Angelina?"

She points to a sitting area in the far corner of the room. There are shoe racks against the wall.

"You can leave your shoes and socks over there, unless you prefer to stay in your socks."

Sweaty feet. Jagged nails. A bent second toe. Callouses in strange configurations. I believe I've covered all these issues, bathed and clipped many times between Amazing Grace and Clair de Lune.

"Then I'll meet you back here, by the Reformer," she adds, pointing to the wooden framed machine behind her. She smiles. It's a funny smile, like we're sharing a private joke, and I hope like hell we are. She turns and I catch a glimpse of her body from behind, well-shaped and strong. The Asian cop is a memory as I take off my shoes and socks then walk to the Reformer.

We are far enough from the other teachers and people training that no one overhears her when she asks, "You are who I think you are, aren't you?" The hint of accusation in her tone. And then, just in case I don't get it, she adds, "Richard, from the dating site."

Caught red-handed, but what did I expect?

"Yes," I answer.

She smiles again. It's far from the belly laugh I'd hoped for.

The class lasts a full hour and it's all business. I am contracted, elongated. Crunched, and my pelvic floor put through its full range of motion. At the conclusion I thank her, and she asks if I'd like to sit and have a glass of water in the area to the front of the studio, next to the shoe racks. There's a vacant sofa and she doesn't have another client for half an hour.

I sit, put my socks and shoes back on as she grabs a bottle of water and two glasses from somewhere behind the desk. If someone were to ask me how I am doing with my new, potential relationship, I would honestly say, "I don't know." Angelina doesn't give much away. What I do know is that I find her very attractive and very professional.

It turns out that she owns the studio, or part-owns the studio; the other part is owned by her ex-husband who wants to be bought out, and she's trying to scrape the money together but it's not easy. I tell her a little about myself, including my recent run-in with the Asian cop and, finally, she laughs; it's a good laugh, restrained but infectious. I laugh too. Oh yes, she knows the Asian cop, at least by sight. According to Angelina, everyone in Santa Barbara knows and fears him. He is without mercy regarding tickets and the scourge of the City College, where he regularly waits in hiding for unsuspecting students to violate the thirty-five mile an hour limit in front of the school. Anything above thirty-seven and he swoops like a two-wheeled hawk.

We talk; we laugh some more. I feel a connection. Twenty minutes goes by in a flutter when finally, I say, "Do I need to book another lesson, or will you let me take you to lunch?" I have learned, from friends in the online dating game, that lunch is a safer request than dinner. Less intimate and less formal, daylight as opposed to candles and moonlight, with no pressure or presumptions of taking it further into the night.

Angelina suggests an alternative. Friends of hers have a blues-rock band and are playing at a local club over the weekend. Would I like to go?

*

The tint peels off, not by me but at the garage of my friend Dutch, who owns a car-detailing business in town. And not till the following week, when his tint-window guy is on the premises. Well, I've got thirty days on the fix it ticket, so I can venture a legal return to Santa Barbara; although I'm hoping my nemesis doesn't ride the nightshift.

I notice a slight change in my demeanor; I'm less excited about what comes next in this mating dance. Fact is, so far, I have not found anything resembling a long-term relationship, and the reason is baggage. There's always something, as all of us seem, for the most part, to be the sum total of our past experiences, and if I can't carry my own baggage, how will I manage anyone else's? I also accept the reality that most of us are wounded, and in some cases, broken. I consider myself in the wounded category, which includes episodes of low self-esteem, and diminished self-belief, translating into a lack of confidence. In plain terms, this means, "Can I fend for myself and survive on my own?" The broken category contains all of the above but is missing the necessary awareness leading to the inner work required to be healthy, and real health requires letting go. Letting go of negative thoughts. Letting go of the past. Dropping the baggage. Lightening up. Living now. All this as the clock ticks and fear bangs at the door. Screaming, "Time is running out!"

For me, talking with my shrink, the Tribal Elder, constitutes some of the inner work, so does spending time alone, along with exercise, prayer and meditation.

Sometimes I wonder why I cannot put the entire dating business on hold until I decree myself strong and healthy enough to actually have a non-dependent relationship, in other words, a relationship where the needs of one do not drain the resources of the other, or become a mutual drain, until the relationship ultimately runs out of resources, and fails.

Addiction is based upon need. Online, or anywhere else. There's never enough, as I pray for Saturday night.

*

It's been a while since I've gone to see live music; once I had a band and I remember the excitement of an audience, and also the nerves I suffered before going on stage. Sort of like the nerves I'm feeling as I park the Volt in my favorite lot and head out onto State Street and into the last light of a summer's day. It's eight o'clock, late by my current standards for a night on the town, but I reckon I'm good till eleven. Dressed casually, my version of the rock 'n roll look, including the Iron & Resin T-shirt and some very old black boots that I've resurrected from my pile of discarded clothing, waiting for a Goodwill collection, and now poised for the dance floor, although my arthritic knee limits my moves to torso twists and pelvic gyrations.

Far from confident as I walk the three blocks from the car park to the club, and there he is. I can't believe it. The Asian cop is seated on his bike and parked on the corner, adjacent to the venue. I've got to walk past him in order to get to the place. Paranoia strikes. What if he remembers me? Demands a viewing of my tinted windows. Arrests me for an infraction of the Santa Barbara dress code, citing the vintage T-shirt or the black boots with their stacked heels? Gives me a citation for being a throwback to the 1980s … Less than fifty yards away when I'm saved by a broken taillight on a Dodge Ram, driven by an unsuspecting bearded guy in a baseball cap. On top of which I believe the Ram may have crossed State Street just as the yellow light turned red. Poor guy. I watch as the thin mouth beneath the helmet draws tight and the visor drops; the motorcycle revs to life, flashers on, pulling menacingly away from the curb; shooting across State Street in pursuit of the Ram, one last shot at misery before sundown. I envision the bearded man in the baseball cap, cuffed and in leg irons or maybe hog-tied and draped over the back of the Honda. Being transported to the lock-up.

Keep walking. I can hear the music, like a blue wave rolling slowly up the street. Recognize "Pride and Joy" by Stevie Ray Vaughn. These guys are good. If I didn't know it was a cover, I'd believe Stevie Ray was alive and playing in Santa Barbara. Walk past the security and through the door. The lights are dim; there's a medium-sized crowd, and several are dancing. I spot Angelina, by herself, moving like a snake in the center of the floor. I love the way she dances. Undulating in slow, sexy rhythms to the bluesy song. I'm too focused to be nervous as I walk towards her. She spots me and motions with her hands, like she wants me to dance with her. It's been a while, like maybe fifteen years, but I can't stop and turn around. No retreat. Closer. She reaches out and puts her hands on my shoulders and guides me. Finding my sea legs. Inhibited. Wish I had a drink. Two drinks. Three. Her eyes are closed. She's not watching me, judging me. No one is. No one cares. Except me. Always watching me. The ego. Always judging. Let it go. I'm moving now. I can feel the beat. Awkward for a while but finally it starts to gel, the guitar cutting right through me, severing the last cords of inhibition. Feeling her body close to mine. Moving. Moving with her. A little more letting go. No one is watching. I'm smiling. She moves closer and kisses me gently on the cheek. Says, "Thanks for showing up." This is it. The moment I've been waiting for. Please, don't let the music end.

Angelina introduces me to the band; we have a couple of glasses of wine, dance some more and the night is over. It's just past eleven when I walk her to her car, with an eye out for the motorcycle cop, who I'm certain would breathalyze us both before issuing a ticket for having too good a time.

At her car, an older BMW, she opens the door, turns towards me and says, "I really had a good evening, thank you." I answer by bending forward and attempting a kiss. She pulls back. Nods her head. Oh God, I've blown it. Swept up by the moment. Here comes that fear again.

"It was good for me, too," I say, trying to cover my awkwardness.

A pause, and she steps forward and kisses me on the lips. It's just a peck but it's something; I suddenly feel elated.

"I'll see you again," she whispers.

Just what I needed to hear. The ego returns. Triumphant.

"Yes, I'll call you," I promise. With that I turn and walk away. My knee hurts from the dancing but I make sure I don't limp, just in case she's watching. Why do I always think that someone is watching?

On State Street and suddenly I'm higher than a kite. I've just discovered a woman that I like, really like, and I believe she likes me too. *Lonely days are gone.*

Then ... the monkey mind kicks in. It's the Tribal Elder, jotting names down on his legal pad, like a group obituary ... Is that Angelina's name? Flashing on all my self-help books with words of surrender and letting go, but I just can't seem to do it. It's a composite of my insights and meditations. My inner voices, babbling, "But you need to spend more time alone. You're not ready for a relationship. You don't even know this person. It's takes a year, maybe two, to get to know someone. You haven't suffered enough. Wait till the shadow monsters bang on the door. Everybody's got baggage. What's hers?" The monkey mind is in full throttle. Finally, launching the zinger. "Wait till she finds out how old you are."

Ouch ... My knee hurts.

Where's that motorcycle cop? I could use a lift to the car park. Riding "bitch."

***

~11~

Our next two dates are at restaurants where my Amex card is given plenty of exercise and I get to hold her hand across the table while she confides that things are not going well with her ex and she may be forced to sell her interest in the Pilates studio, which is the single thing, except for her five cats and twin daughters, that she cherishes most in life. "Pilates is just who I am," she says. I suppress an enormous urge to become her rescuer, but restrain, stay quiet and allow her to vent. There are tears; soulful tears running from those beautiful brown eyes.

We are now over two months into our relationship and have only kissed, although the kisses have progressed to slight tongue touching, but a far cry from English Rose and her Loch Ness monster. So far, so good, I tell myself.

I also tell the Tribal Elder, trying to curb my enthusiasm so as to avoid the manifestation of the legal pad and Angelina's name being added to the list of the departed. Interpreting the pad as an equivalent to "the hook" which in vaudevillian days was a curtain hook extended from backstage, intended to pull the performer away, generally by the neck, to put an end to an overlong or boring act.

"Go slowly," he advises. "Be patient, see where it leads."

Slowly has never been an attribute of mine. Neither has patience. I seem to have fast twitch in my psyche. Besides, I'm a seventy-year-old man, who Angelina still thinks is sixty-two, a fact

I have never mentioned to the Elder. Despite what Mick Jagger says, time is definitely not on my side.

"But she is very different from the others," I say, in my most calm and assured voice. Then, spoken like a true adult. "I love her."

His blue eyes seem to change focus as he swipes a hand through his longish straw-colored hair then observes me with compassion.

Oh no, I've done it, I think, as he reaches across to his table. Fingers on the pad, lifting it.

"Come on," I plead. "Give me a break."

He flicks through a few pages until he locates "the list." Looking down at it.

"I believe you also loved Michelle from Pasadena, then there was English Rose, but that was only a minor flirtation, and Janine, a local lady who you saw briefly before Suzanne, also known as The Seeker, and I've written something here that looks like Amazing Grace… but crossed her out for some reason." He pauses and looks up at me; his eyes sharp and focused. I feel like a rabbit, in the sights of a hunting hawk, with nowhere to hide. "And, of course, your ex-wife, any dreams of her lately?"

"No."

So far, he hasn't picked up his pencil, or pen.

"Has there been any physical intimacy with … Angelina?"

"A kiss."

"That's it, and you've been seeing her for two months?"

"Yes."

"Slow, for you, isn't it?"

"I haven't wanted to push it."

"What makes you say you love her?"

"It's a feeling."

"Describe the feeling."

"I like being around her."

There's a long pause. He checks his watch, lays down the pad. Stands up from the chair. We hug, with my head on his shoulder.

"This could be good for you," he says.

I feel like the Elder has given me his blessings, which is important, since at this time I am very susceptible to the thoughts and words of others.

I turn to exit when he adds, "But be careful."

*

The next trip to Santa Barbara is a big one. To Angelina's house and it includes meeting her twin daughters and five cats; it also includes me clearing up the business about my age. Age has been weighing heavily on me and in spite of Oatmeal Jane's insistence that everyone online lies, my lie has become a burden, conflicting with my self-help principle of being impeccable with my words, including no self-deceit and no deceiving others. I ask how I'd feel if the shoe were on the other foot, if Angelina confessed to being sixty-one and not fifty-three. Not great. Trust is important. I need to tell the truth. And I may need a few glasses of wine to do it.

I'm seventy. Seventy-years "young." Yeah, right. Young man, may I help you carry your groceries to the car?

Her place is modest but tasteful, a three-bedroom shingled house on Mountain Avenue, on the more affordable west side of town. Inside is a mixture of expensive and practical, a well-used wrap-around sofa, occupied by three of her five cats, cabinets containing objects of art, hand-blown glass and small sculptures in silver and gold, and a couple of hand-carved wooden chairs that I think may be Mexican. All sitting on a large, red Afghan carpet. Angelina explains that the eclectic assortment of furniture and collectibles are remnants from her past marriage. I surmise that someone had very good taste and a fair amount of money.

Enter the twins. Twenty-two years old, beautiful, with their mother's hair and brown eyes, and very hip with their ankle tattoos and bell bottom retro jeans. They are in and out quickly, leaving for a party, so I barely have time for a hug and a hello before they are gone and I'm sitting with a glass of wine on the sofa. One of the cats, a great bushy female named Cleo who looks like a Maine Coon cat but half the size, sort of like the motorcycle cop, nudges closer and ends up in my lap. I consider this a promising sign. Meaning that if Angelina's daughters hug me and Cleo, with her lion's mane of fur, trusts me enough to sit in my lap, I'm nearly part of the household, which is something I've been missing since mine broke up. It's that feeling of family, an intimate connection to a group. Five minutes at Angelina's is not a replacement but it's enough to remind me of what it felt like, the love and the security.

Angelina is in the kitchen, which is just off the main room. Cooking. Cooking for us. It's some kind of chicken dish with rice and it smells good, makes me feel warm and fuzzy. All of this plays straight into my needs. Suddenly, relaxed from the wine and soothed by Cleo's gentle purrs, I'm home again.

And what does "home" mean?

For me, home is a place with no stress, where all my adult worries wash away. I feel there is someone there to look after me. It's a feeling. A nostalgia. I remember my mom and dad and my visits home to Philadelphia after I'd moved to London. Warm fires, Mom cooking and Dad sipping a Manhattan, or playing his violin, then going upstairs to my bedroom; the same room I had as a kid. That feeling of home, but that was *Yesterday,* and all my troubles were far away.

Angelina and I eat at a table outside, under the light of a new moon, another glass of wine, turn on some music, and there's Van Morrison, as if by divine intervention, singing "Brown-Eyed Girl." Sometimes the heavens seem to open up and talk to us but it's how we listen that makes all the difference. Everything seems so right with Angelina. But am I listening?

She is an orphan. Adopted by an older couple who found the actuality of raising a baby girl more than they had bargained on. Returned to the orphanage. Another adoption. This time, one of six children on an Iowa farm. Not much love. No dad with a Manhattan and a violin. No bedroom cocoon to hide away in. Instead, bunk beds, up at dawn, hard work and a strict Catholic discipline. Feelings of abandonment. A runaway by sixteen, tending bars illegally, working her way towards California, the promised land. Hustling as a "go-go" girl in West Hollywood, showing her breasts for an extra twenty bucks stuffed down her jeans. Picked up by a red-hot car salesman, living large on Rovers and Bentleys. Big house in the hills. All the drugs. All the thrills.

Am I listening?

Or am I projecting everything I need onto this person in front of me? She's young, compared to me, pretty, exuding love and tenderness.

God, I want to kiss her.

A slow song comes on. It's Van the Man again, singing "Have I told You Lately."

She stands up and begins to move. I watch her in the moonlight. What does she look like naked, with her strong legs and rounded hips? What would it feel like to wake up beside her? I stand and gently take hold of her hand. Spirit and music merge in a timeless space, and we're dancing. I can feel her breathing. Stars above, pulsating in the black sky. Emotions welling inside me. Tears that I won't let out. Making me aware of how raw I am. "Love yourself," the Elder says, but my needs are gaping; it's so much easier to love the woman standing in front of me and forget about myself. So much easier to forget the inner work, like honesty and integrity. Keep on dancing.

I never get around to the issue of my age, why ruin the evening?

*

You can resign from the dating sites, but the dating sites won't resign from you. Stop payment and cancel your membership, explain in one of their online forms that you are leaving because you have found a partner; they will still send you email notifications of messages, tempting you to take a look, see who likes you. Maybe there is someone better than the "human" being you have found, someone with less baggage or a more compatible set of suitcases full of the past. It's tempting to look. Tempting to see what the other has to say. Does it resonate? Ring a bell?

I cancel. Take myself off all three sites.

The messages continue.

I hit delete, although sometimes it's difficult. So curious to see the face of the person who has seen my face, read my words, and is interested in connecting with me.

What happens if things don't work out with Angelina?

I sense the fear of a freefall into empty space, the unknown, the void of being alone again, but I'm alone now, and just don't know it.

*

We take a five-hour road trip, up the old Pacific Coast Highway to Big Sur, with its giant Redwoods, some reaching as high as three hundred and fifty feet, and its dramatic cliff-edged coastline. Stay in a romantic cabin, with a log fire and twin beds. Twin beds because we've both agreed to get to know each other before we become lovers. It wasn't my idea, but it makes sense … in a Victorian kind of way. So, we have a glass of wine, then another, and Angelina has a couple more. I'm beginning to notice that she drinks more than I do. But that's okay; I'm not a heavy drinker, two glasses of wine are my usual limit. It's her business. Not for me to comment. We talk, about our children, about her business. She's tight for money and the ex-husband is not coming through. I'm starting to think of how I can help. Problem is, I don't have much. Enough to hold me over till I reinvent myself, either as a writer or a personal trainer, but not enough to bail her out.

We talk some more. Kiss a little. Sip a bit more of the Big Sur Red. Have a little cuddle, and that's it; she goes to her bed while I stay in mine. No protest. We talk some more from our respective safe havens. It's a big boy pajama party. Giggles. Laughter. Feels so good to laugh. Such a great release. Trust. We're building it.

And then … Talking about our kids and I mention, in the relaxed flow of conversation, that I was really pushing it to have my first son at fifty-one and my next at fifty-four. Wondering if I'd attend their high-school graduation on a walker. My laughter fills the room, until I notice that I'm the only one laughing.

Silence, except for the crackle of the oak in the dying fire.

"How old did you say they are?" she asks. Her voice is restrained.

I don't know how to begin. Wondering what happens next? Does she exit? Out into the night and the canopy of the Redwoods, or maybe she'll demand a solo cabin? Have I just ended my romance? I've got a hollow feeling that seems to extend from my feet to the crown of my head.

No room to lie here, no room for anything but honesty. Why didn't I tell her that night on her back porch? Why didn't I change my date of birth on the website? Vanity. Fear. What happened to being impeccable with my words? Okay, Oatmeal Jane, you got me into this, talk to me. What now?

I feel like I'm in a confessional. About to admit to a mortal sin. Repent? Yes, absolutely.

Attempting to keep the solemnity from my voice, I answer, "My oldest is nineteen and my youngest is sixteen."

I listen, believing I hear her mental calculator adding and subtracting numbers.

And finally, her voice, clear as a temple bell.

"Richard … That makes you seventy."

*

"Yes, I am seventy years old." Hard for me to believe, even harder to say. I remember when my dad turned seventy. He was five years into his retirement and at a loss as to what to do with his time, so the Manhattans grew stronger and the violin seemed to play the same old tune, every night at six. Sometimes, I'd see him wandering around on the front porch, puffing his pipe and talking to himself. Very animated, using his hands to make a point. I had no idea what he was saying, and he probably didn't either, but I loved the smell of the burning tobacco. Twelve years later, the pipe that he had substituted for cigarettes because he thought it was safer, caught up with his lungs and it was over. In the blink of an eye.

Angelina's voice brings me back to the log cabin.

"Why did you lie?"

The fire has died, and the room seems very still, just two disjointed voices filing the dark space.

I think of Oatmeal Jane and her daughter. Dropping me in it while meaning me well. Things seemed much more of a game back then. But now, after several years of failed dates with too many dinners, lunches, cups of coffee and "meaningful" chatter, the game's become tedious, and sometimes desperate. I want the game to end.

"It's a long story," I reply. "The fact is, I wonder if you would have ever sent me a message if you knew my real age."

"Do you think age has anything to do with our connection?"

"I'm not sure."

"Lying does," she says.

"I am sorry."

There's a lengthy pause and I'm feeling totally vulnerable. Suddenly, we are strangers again, lying side by side in the void.

Then, just as I am about to declare to myself that all is lost, I hear a faint noise, like a child's laughter, more a giggle. Then a voice, small and girlish, "Grandpa?"

"Did you just call me Grandpa?"

"Yes …. Grandpa."

And she starts to laugh. It's contagious. Soon, we are both laughing, so hard my sides hurt.

"Grandpa," I repeat between guffaws. "I am not a grandpa."

And then she's in bed with me, soft smooth skin, warm and naked.

"Prove it," she says.

***

~12~

The relationship continues as I am slowly integrated into the family of girls and cats, with home-cooked dinners, glasses of wine, shots of tequila and the occasional hit from the family bong.

My sons are supportive but somewhat skeptical, the oldest being the most outspoken.

"Take your time, Dad," he advises. "I really like Angelina, but there's something a little crazy about her."

Crazy? What does he mean by that? I ask and he can't quite explain, saying it's just a feeling.

I attempt to reassure everyone, including myself, by inviting Angelina to visit the Tribal Elder. Considering it courageous on her part when she accepts the invitation.

At one point during the very relaxed hour, the Elder asks her, "What do you fear most in this relationship?"

Without hesitation, she answers, "That Richard will leave me."

That makes no sense. I've never done anything to suggest I'd leave. Leaving is the last thing on my mind.

"Why would he do that?" the Elder asks.

Angelina begins to sob.

"I don't know."

I've heard that before, when I asked my ex-wife why she was leaving. "I don't know. I don't know. I don't know." The most frustrating three words in the English language.

And I don't get it. Is there something I've missed, something that my son has seen that I have avoided?

The session ends and we leave, back to my house, for two shots of tequila for Angelina, and a quiet chat on the sofa.

"I'm not going anywhere," I say.

She looks at me. Her eyes are so deep, like I can see her soul, but whose soul am I looking at, whose soul am I trying to find?

She cries and I hug her, feeling heroic, like I am saving her; or is she saving me?

If I hold on tight enough, she'll never go; or I'll never leave.

Am I paying attention?

Am I?

The episode with the Elder is slowly buried beneath dinners, listening to music and walks on the beach. I'm in love. It's a feeling, full of energy. Like a teenager, standing on my head, showing off, running into the ocean with my clothes on. Making love in the backseat of my car. Getting caught by the beach patrol. Yes, that's me. Seventy, going on seventeen.

Loaning her twenty thousand dollars to pay off her ex and own the Pilates studio. Yes, I do that too.

Do I have the money? Not really. Do I need to rescue Angelina? Absolutely. Am I trying to rescue myself? No doubt.

Angelina promises to pay me back, support me with her earnings, take care of me for the rest of my life. Love me forever.

Am I listening?

Yes, and I'm hearing what I want to hear.

My birthday comes and Angelina, the most grateful girl on the planet, has a surprise for me. Be at her house by 8 o'clock. The twins are away for the weekend so come prepared to spend the night. Her telephone voice has a mischievous quality.

*

By now, I am, for the most part, enjoying my new freedom. Yes, there are times of fear and negativity, usually at 3 AM, when worries about health, aging and money, particularly after my twenty-thousand-dollar rescue, become magnified and the specter of death hovers in the ether just above my bed; and there are times when I re-examine my failed marriage, wondering why I didn't see my ex-wife's unhappiness and regret that we didn't talk enough, that I took so much for granted. And there are times when I look down the long driveway and see my sons waving goodbye. Then I mourn the break-up of my family, but I am learning to accept the present. And also, to accept the fact that the boys must grow, become men, strong and independent. I meditate regularly and discipline myself to replace fear with love and gratitude for what the universe is giving me.

Love and gratitude, the true antidote for anxiety and fear. It's a tough discipline.

Angelina is a gift, at least I want to see her that way.

But, through the work I've done with the Elder, and my reading and studying of self-help and psychology books, I know that Angelina is also part projection. There's more than a hint of my lost self in that free-spirited, dancing brown-eyed girl who I'm fairly certain sneaks a shot or two of tequila at mid-day. Reminiscent of my days in the late sixties and early seventies, when life was more carefree, with everything ahead and no fear of the future; there's something wild and untamed about Angelina, far removed from the disciplined Pilates teacher who led me through that first class at her studio. She is that, but she is also something else, and with time, she's coming clearer into focus.

At fifty-three, she still looks young to me. Nice to sit across from her in a candlelit restaurant. Not a line or wrinkle in her pretty face. Is that my face? My projection of youth.

Am I healthy enough to keep this real?

Angelina is also a lesson, and, at this point, I'm not sure what that lesson is.

One thing for certain, she has filled in that feeling of "something is missing," that faint melancholia and, for that, I'm grateful.

*

I arrive at eight, park in the street and exit my car. Candles flicker in the windows of the small, shingled house; I anticipate a romantic evening. Maybe she's cooked dinner, one of her wonderful chicken dishes. We will sit out on the back porch; make love in the hammock, beneath the moon and stars. What a wonderful way to celebrate another year or life. I walk to her front door; I can hear music playing from inside. Sounds like rhythm and blues, something soulful from the '80s. Listen closer and hear Marvin Gaye singing, *Mercy, mercy me.* ... I knock. Can't wait to get inside. Get back to that feeling of being home, because that's what Angelina's house has become to me, a home, with children and laughter and food on the table. And warmth, and love. I hear footsteps from beyond the door. Get ready to hug her. Hear the chain come off its hook. The bolt turns and the door opens; a bleached blonde woman stands in front of me.

Who are you? I wonder, but remain silent, staring at the oversized fake breasts with white pasties covering the nipples, the laced thong, black stockings and red high heels. In the background, Angelina is dancing, doing her snaky dance; eyes closed and lost in the rhythms.

The smell of marijuana wafts like an earthy incense.

I carefully navigate my way past the gigantic orbs and walk inside.

Angelina hands me a glass of tequila. Enough to induce a general anesthesia.

"Richard, this is Nanette. We used to work together in Hollywood."

"Hi," Nanette whispers, hugs me then plants a wet collagen-laced kiss on my lips.

Angelina follows up with a joint the size of a small cigar. I take a token hit and head for the sofa. Where's Cleo, my security cat? Sink into the soft cushion. "Come on, man, relax," I tell myself, "This is love in the twenty-first century. Stop being so uptight." After all, it's my birthday.

Half a tumbler of tequila later and another pull on the cigar-sized joint and I'm easy enough to allow Nanette to sit on my lap; she has removed her thong and is proudly describing the new clitoral piercing that her husband, a sergeant in the Army on active duty, gave her for her fiftieth birthday. The thought of giving a clitoral piercing as a birthday gift defies my imagination. I must really be out of date. She leans back and using her fingers, displays it, a small titanium rod; it resembles a miniature barbell.

"Wow ... Yes ... That's really nice." Trying to act nonchalant, thinking that maybe if I'd lavished my ex-wife with such treasures, she wouldn't have left.

"Your turn, Richard," Angelina says, going to the shelf above the amplifier. Lifting down a silver box, big enough to hold a bottle of cologne, and tied with a red bow. She dances forward, skirts around Nanette, and places the silver box in my hands. Nanette stands up and Angelina removes her blouse and bra, freeing her natural full breasts. With the music playing and both women swaying topless above me the moment takes on a ceremonial feel, like I'm part of some tribal ritual. Great anticipation and all eyes are on me as I untie the bow and rip through the shiny paper.

Looking down at the box with the black and white instructions printed on the cover; I can see the contents through the plastic top.

Speechless. My God! Just what I've always wanted.

Finally, I say, "Thank you." Staring at the matt black, electric cock ring.

"Do you want to try it on?" Nanette asks.

I look up; both women are looking down at the birthday boy with his new toy. My mind is spinning, the monkey mind whirling with clichés, questions and proclamations. "I'm too old for this kind of shit. Am I supposed to have sex with both of them, is that what Angelina wants? Does she really love me? Why would she do this? Is it a test? Is she crazy? Am I crazy? Wouldn't most men want this? Isn't this a man's fantasy? Am I too straight for the modern world? I don't want to be here. I want a home-cooked dinner. A Manhattan with a maraschino cherry on top. My guitar. Hello Dad. Hello Mom. Where's my old bedroom? Where's Cleo? I want to go home. How do I get out?"

"I think I'll wait till later," I answer, not wanting to break up the ceremony or offend the natives.

The music ends and the women sit down, both topless, and conversation continues, as if naked and topless is a natural way to spend a birthday. Welcome to the nudist colony, anyone for badminton?

Turns out that Nanette is traveling, lap dancing from LA to Georgia, working her way through topless bars from state to state. Yes, she's in her fifties, but cosmetic surgery has smoothed her face enough that she can pass for thirty in the dim lights of a nightclub. Earning a couple of thousand on a good shift, and hardly anything on a bad one. It all depends on the crowd, how far she goes with the lap dance and how generous the recipient feels. It's a tough life for a middle-aged woman, but she's been doing it for so long it's the only life she knows, particularly with no children and her husband away for such long periods of time.

The more she talks, the more I see beyond the projection of the bleached-blonde stripper with the party-sized chest and, once again, I'm looking at a human face with a human story. I commend her husband for letting her be who she is. Talk about letting go, he must be a master. Either that, or he doesn't care enough to stop it. So many types of relationships out there, functional and dysfunctional. Keeps bringing me back to what am I looking for, and what do I need?

Angelina slides closer to me; we kiss once as Nanette watches. I sense a longing in Nanette, maybe for some real affection, something honest and true, and, as the kiss ends and our lips part, I sense her loneliness; it must be tough, going from town to town, sitting on strangers' laps, listening to drunken voices, bathed in breath that reeks of sugary margaritas. Fondled by strange hands.

My birthday present remains virginal in its box.

Ten o'clock and I'm tired. Time for bed but the girls seem to be revving up for more action, fueled by tequila and grass; Nanette is demonstrating some advanced lap techniques, and I am the designated lap. I'd really prefer Cleo, but she's too smart and probably sound asleep on an old mattress in the backyard shed.

One more round of "She Works Hard for the Money" by Donna Summer, and I move from the sofa and shuffle towards the front door.

"Where are you going?" Angelina asks, raspy shades of tequila coloring her voice.

"I've had a great time, but I want my bed," I reply.

"But ..."

"Thank you. It's been a wonderful party." I hold up the box containing the cock ring. "And what a fantastic gift."

Wave goodbye, and head for my car. Pulling out I get a sad feeling, like the distance between Angelina and me has just grown.

Up the long driveway to my empty house, a little closer to who I am, and a little less sure of whether Angelina and I will work out in the long run. It hurts to think this way, because I want a companion, someone to trust and care for, and who will trust and care for me. But it's honest, and finally, honesty is all we've got.

And honestly, I'm fed up with online dating.

***

Know when to walk away and know when to run ....

Don Schlitz, echoing the oft repeated words of the Tribal Elder, wrote those lyrics for a song titled "The Gambler," in 1973, and country singer Kenny Rogers made them famous.

He's singing about the game of poker, and when it's time to fold the cards and walk away from the table, when it's time to hold them, and when it's time to run; but he could as easily be singing about love.

In love, the high card is the heart. Rule number one: Don't wear it on your sleeve, which I do frequently and have done for most of my life. Too easy to read. Too easy to play, but when I'm in, I'm in, and, in spite of all the warning signs, I'm still in with Angelina.

I send friends to her Pilates studio, trying to help build business. Several come back and report that they smelled alcohol on her breath. One of them is specific: "It was tequila." I don't want to believe this person; in fact, I find it annoying, like maybe she is trying to undermine my relationship. Still, I confront Angelina, and she denies it. "I'm too professional for that," she says, angry that I would even ask. I believe her; because I want to believe her.

Her behavior becomes more erratic. She cries easily, and quarrels with her daughters. But I'm guilty, too. Sometimes, I'll have a shot of tequila with her in the afternoon. It feels like a secret bond, a relaxing intimacy. Encouraging long soulful kissing while buffering that honest inner voice that spoke to me on the night of the matt black cock ring; it is unlikely that Angelina and I will last, not at the pace we're going.

Am I listening?

No, not really, I've shoved the truth into the background, too frightened to call a spade, a spade. Yet knowing, at least intellectually, that without the inner work, we are destined to repeat our life's lessons, traveling in long, painful circles right back to the beginning. Round and round we go again.

I am in denial.

Telling myself this relationship will get better, but not doing anything that's necessary to improve it, and that begins with the self. Both our selves. Communicating.

Am I learning?

No, I'm writing, again, but even that is an old book that was never published and I'm simply adding a few final chapters. Is that my life, an old book in need of an ending? But it makes me feel like I'm working, when the thing I am really working on is my denial mechanism. Whatever it is I have with Angelina, and it's been nearly a year, I don't want it to end. Frightened of the void. That loneliness. That feeling of "I'll never find another." Quiet desperation.

Angelina invites me to dinner, then when I am on the highway, halfway to Santa Barbara, she tells me not to come. Why? I'm not certain. Something I've said? I ask; she doesn't know, not exactly, but what she does know is that we are not meant to be together; she knows I am not "the one." She tells me this several times as I exit the freeway and head homewards, back to the long, dark driveway. The one? Who is the one, and what is the one supposed to do? Rescue her? Rescue me? I've tried. It doesn't work, because with each rescue another crisis is created, a new drama, because there is never enough rescue, and always another wound. Here he comes, King Richard the Lionhearted, storming down the stone stairway to Angelina's dungeon, full of man-eating shadows. Holding out a giant torch. Illuminating each of them; shadows that date all the way back to the orphanage. Confronting them one by one with his golden sword, while stopping occasionally for a double shot of Cuervo Gold, a hit on the bong, and a roll in the hay.

But ... King Richard has his own shadows, and he hasn't been dealing with them. Not lately. Why? Because he's in love or doing his best rendition of love. Into his first long-term relationship since his marriage, and he's not giving an inch of space away, the space it would take to know himself a little bit better. He's not letting go, and he's sure not running.

Words from the Elder: We are each other's teachers; we subconsciously choose our lessons, then wonder why it hurts so much. No pain, no gain? Labor pains. Suffering. Giving birth is an exquisite suffering, because we are giving birth to the authentic self. "But... Please, doctor, I beg you, may I have an epidural..? Come on, just to get me through."

*

Angelina and I trim the Christmas tree. It's a circus of lights, laughter, and that feeling of belonging again, that feeling of home. Tequila and a new strain of sativa picked up at the local dispensary elevate the event to a full-on party, with just the two of us. I've never been happier.

Out to dinner, candlelight, everything is warm, talk about the kids, admire her new haircut, hold hands across the table. We leave the restaurant; I walk her to her car. We kiss softly; make plans for the holidays. Fifteen minutes passes and I receive a call. She's pulled over by the side of the road. Crying so hard she can't see what's in front of her. Why is she so upset? What could have changed so drastically in fifteen minutes? Sobbing down the phone. She's broke. She has no medical insurance. The studio is folding. She's suffering a catastrophic disease. Then says she isn't but could be; it's possible.

I listen; she touches something inside me, love, compassion, fear of the void, the pain. She loves me, as well as she can; cooks creamy garlic chicken in a blue carbon steel wok and makes love in an outdoor hammock while her kids watch TV inside. She has given me a home, warmth, a surrogate family, a place to go at the end of the day. I have discontinued therapy. Declared myself healed.

And now, Angelina is in distress. So, what do I do? ...

I invite her to move in with me. I mean, what else is there to do?

Into my house. My sanctuary. Yes. That will be just perfect. Solve everything.

Why?

Because I love her.

Run... Sorry, Kenny, I know I've got a bad hand, but I'm not folding. In fact, I'm going all in.

Why?

Because she loves me.

... Really?

Angelina declines my offer, claiming that marauding coyotes may eat her cats.

The relationship continues.

She breaks up with me every other evening, often by telephone, because "you're not the one," and makes up with me on alternate evenings, because "I'm in love with you." Break-up, make-up, like clockwork.

I'm living on a roller-coaster.

Clair de Lune, "Star of heaven, send your light on me."

My agent says my new/old book stinks. My ex-publisher confirms it. Rejected. Failed. I'm hurt, angry, confrontational; but, finally, I am honest. Both men are right. They've seen through me. The book is contrived; I've been going through the motions. Filling pages with words, competent but uninspired; and art, real art, cannot be contrived. It flows from the heart to the page, using the writer as a portal. Characters drawn from experience, defined with words, and fact or fiction, those words must speak honestly.

Am I listening?

How honest have I been?

Stressed out, I suffer what appears to be a mini stroke during one of my breathing classes at the yoga studio. Standing in front of a group of nine people, dizzy, babbling, unable to make my brain connect with my tongue. It's terrifying to be so... Disconnected.

Off to the ER. Tests show no cerebral damage, and no one can be certain what actually happened; maybe a pinched carotid artery during one of my movements, maybe a piece of loose plaque blocking a blood vessel; but it's a wake-up call. I'm mortal. I am going to die. Just a question of when. But can I get my love-life intact before the next incarnation?

Angelina picks me up from the hospital, drives me home, promises to look after me, push my wheelchair, give me body washes, enemas and change my diapers.

I book an emergency session with the Tribal Elder.

I talk about Angelina. He listens. I cry. He offers me Kleenex. I shout angrily. He takes my blood pressure —180/90 — tells me to take a few long, slow breaths. I calm down — 125/80. He inhales deeply, meets my eyes, looks at me with a fatherly compassion and says, "Run," which must be sound advice since it rings in unison with the lyrics from "The Gambler."

Stubbornly, I still will not leave the table. Play another hand. Just one more. It's got to get better. Be lucky. More dinners, more U-turns on the way to her house, more proclamations of love, and finally the penultimate showdown. It takes place at my place, following my own rendition of creamy garlic chicken, slightly dry, and a bottle of rosé.

I'm not sure what sets her off, possibly the mention of her studio and the dwindling client list, possibly because I am not "the one," but she's at full-throttle quicker than my longed-for Tesla, except this time I'm prepared, this time it's me who issues the ultimatum.

"Get out," I say. 'Just, get out."

She appears stunned.

"I've never said this to you before, Angelina, but I mean it, get your things and leave."

I've always been on the other side of this exchange but this time I am the aggressor. It feels liberating.

"Angelina, please… Go."

Suddenly she seems smaller, like a schoolgirl being disciplined by the headmaster. Walking to the bathroom to get her toothbrush and hair dryer, a few bits of clothing and a shawl in my bedroom. I walk beside her, struggling not to call the whole thing off, or laugh, pretending it's a joke, but I don't, because it is not a joke and our relationship has become a repetitive circle, like a ring of fire, incinerating both of us. I open the drawer beneath the sink and remove my birthday present.

"And, don't forget this," I say, handing her the cock ring.

That brings on the tears, as if I had just thrown our wedding band into the toilet. Sobbing, cock ring in hand, she exits the house, climbs into her BMW and drives away, accompanied by the sound of crunching gravel, grinding the still night air.

I sit down on the sofa. The house seems very quiet, very still, as if peace has finally returned after a long and ugly war. I don't feel the void, not yet, but I am slightly shell-shocked. After a year, she's gone. I loved her, still do, but it was not a healthy love. Perhaps neither of us were ready; too many wounds, too much insecurity. I recall the woman I first met at the Pilates studio, professional and restrained, then think of the woman I knew a year later, after the shadows had climbed the steps from the dungeon, pounding on the door, finally crashing through. Shrieking like banshees, "We're gonna' destroy everything you've got."

Will I ever see her again?

The phone calls begin at eleven o'clock at night. I don't answer. They continue without stop for half an hour, twenty, twenty-four calls. Finally, Angelina leaves a message, "Why are you doing this? Why are you so cruel?"

I almost pick up on the next ring, but I have nothing to say; there's no argument here, no room for compromise. Together, we will only recreate this situation, in different forms, over and over again. I know that much from therapy. The alternative is more inner work. How long does it take to give birth to yourself? This is agony.

"Be patient," says the Elder.

*

I am in my bed, staring at the ceiling at 3 AM when I hear the sound, again, tires against gravel, directly below my window. My room is illuminated by headlights. Then darkness as a car door slams. I realize I have not locked my house. Footsteps in the living room. Someone charging up the staircase, moving light and fast.

It's Angelina. She has removed her flip-flops, skirt and bra, leaving only her red thong, one of three I gave her for Christmas: it's a home invasion by Victoria's Secret.

"Grandpa." Did she just call me Grandpa?

She's in my bed. No protest from me. I'm overwhelmed. Too old to fight. Too weak to resist. We make love; its intense but over quickly, and as fast as she arrived, she's gone.

"That's it!" she shouts, descending the staircase, two steps at a time. "Hope it was good for you, cause that's the last you'll ever see me, Grandpa!"

***

~13~

Tears are a purge. It has been said that tears are years, a blessed stress release, a pain-drain. If I was seventy-one when I started crying, I reckon I'm about fifty-five when I stop. Sad and forlorn, everything from Angelina to my mini stroke has flooded my system and come out through my eyes.

I loved Angelina. Still do, but neither of us has done the work required for a healthy relationship; in fact, I'm uncertain as to whether either of us understands what that work entails.

A month passes, then another; the driveway looks like the long lonesome road again, except there's a new car in front of my door. The ecologically friendly Volt is gone and a black, Infiniti Q60 has taken its place. Low and fast and sleek, with eight thousand miles on the clock and an older, wiser man at the wheel, still determined to find what he's looking for.

Nights are long. There's an owl outside my window; "hoo-hooing," alone in the night, reminding me of that Hank Williams song, *'I'm So Lonesome I Could Cry'*; featuring a lonely whippoorwill, who sounds to blue to fly, and a far-way whistle from a midnight train, as *time goes crawling by*. Written when I was four years old, sixty-seven years ago. Gone. In the blink of an eye.

*

Back to the Elder and a seat on the sofa. Here it comes, the legal pad, this time with a pen. I notice he's using the Bic ballpoint, different from his fountain pen, which I assume is a collector's item from his Jungian days and reserved, perhaps, for marriage break-ups, or the pencil which is erasable if things change for the better. No, this one is ink, indelible, but doesn't involve alimony or

family, so I get the Bic.

"Angelina," he says, writing down her name as if it is an incurable disease and not to be trifled with. Then he looks across the divide at me. "She was wounded."

"Why didn't we talk about it at the time, after you'd met her?"

"Some things have to be experienced," he answers.

"And me, am I still wounded?"

"You're getting better," he assures.

"But I'm miserable," I say.

"You're grieving."

I think of Angelina. I had high hopes. There was so much about the relationship that felt right. And then, it fell apart, bit by bit, shot by shot. Pass me the Cuervo Gold. Maybe I could have saved it. Pass me the Kleenex.

"There was nothing you could do for her," the Elder continues. "She has to do it for herself. We all do."

"Yes, but I seem to be in a constant state of grieving, for one thing or another."

"And why do you think that is?"

"Me," I admit. "I'm grieving for me."

"Well ... You've been through a rough patch."

"I'd just like the roller coaster to end," I say. "I'd like to find a stable relationship and get on with my life. I'm going broke taking women to dinner and driving hundreds of miles to meet someone that I have no connection with. I'm obsessed with the internet and who likes me, or who sends me a message, and I may be a sex addict."

"Stability is within you, no one gives it to you," he answers, "but you already know that, and the relationship with yourself is the one you are developing, but it's slow, and it can be painful. Regarding sex, the fact that you think about it and engage in it shows that you are not depressed. You are not a sex addict." Then, just to make sure, he looks down at the list. "Active, but not an addict. Not at this point, anyway."

I depart with a hug and a promise that I am a greatly improved human being, facing my aloneness and becoming more individuated. The Elder has confidence in me. I feel inspired, on the verge of some great breakthrough as I walk to my car. My cell phone is waiting for me on the passenger seat, which is where I usually leave it during therapy sessions. I pick it up, press the button, and spot a new email, a message from the dating site. About to hit delete when I see the small thumbnail-sized photo accompanying the notification. Her screen name is Ice Maiden and she's beautiful, in a blonde Nordic kind of way, sparkling blue eyes, high cheekbones and a celebrity smile, wide and white. Smiling straight at me.

Is this my reward for successfully completing this phase of my inner work?

I'm ready.

*

After months of sending photos and notifications, the dating site has finally hooked me again. I can't get access to Ice Maiden's message without renewing my membership. It's strange, even with something as seemingly as remote as online dating, it can be a name, eyes, a smile, a turn of phrase, something, but when it grabs me, I'm drawn back into the game. Willing to spend $29.99 a month to find out what she has written. Hoping for more than "hi."

Her message is simple and to the point. "Hello, I have read your profile and you sound interesting. What kind of books do you write?" It's signed Kristan.

I answer. "Thrillers and memoirs, but none recently. Seem to be stuck for a good idea. Do you have any?"

The following evening, I'm deep into a telephone conversation with a Norwegian woman; her online age is fifty-six years old and her profession is given as a veterinary acupuncturist, in other words she acupunctures animals. In an effort to relate, I tell her that I sometimes dog sit for a Chihuahua named Penny, owned by my friend Ingrid; Penny bites everyone but me. No one knows why, but Penny and I seem to share a secret bond, and she has seen me through some rough, anxious nights, cuddled close to me in my bed, in the spoon position. Kristan laughs and says that

Chihuahuas are tricky to acupuncture because of their nervous temperament. I'm more feeling her words than listening. Attracted to her accent, her *w*'s sound like *v*'s, and "Norway" comes out as "Norvay" which, for some reason, I find sexy. She lives in Santa Ynez, which is a beautiful little cowboy town, with saloons and horses tied to hitching posts, and a population of about four thousand, about half the population of my town, so it's no wonder she's online. Kristan is also about sixty-five miles away, or about an hour and a half drive. I'm used to that; everywhere in California is an hour's drive, or more, and people spend a good portion of their lives in cars, wheeling down the highways or sitting in traffic. Dividing time between work, traveling, texting and scouring the dating sites.

The phone call is easy; our tastes in music are similar and we talk about blues singers and guitarists. She has no children, which is a plus, since other people's children can equate to heavy baggage, plus I have two of my own. Divorced and owns her own home, which means she's not digging for mine. Cynical as this sounds, I'm beginning to hear between the lines. Detecting vocal intonations, women fishing for money or being deceitful, like being in the middle of, and not actually divorced. Dragging the new match right into the matrimonial mess. Vetting by phone is a process called survival.

After two hours of banter, we agree to meet for dinner, not coffee or lunch, which means we both think this match has some potential.

"Oh, by the way," I add as an afterthought. "I'm closer to seventy than sixty. I've tried to change it online, but the site won't let me. If that's a problem, I understand."

"I'm actually fifty-eight," she answers. "And I'll drive to you."

*

It's a rainy Friday night, eight o'clock, and I'm seated in a quiet Italian restaurant about two miles from my home, at a table close to a big fireplace and a roaring log fire. Wearing jeans, a green linen shirt and sipping a glass of red wine, slowly, trying to relax in preparation for Kristan's arrival.

She texts; according to her Nav, she's ten minutes away. Sip a little more. No matter how many times I do this, I get nervous. It's that first impression. That first handshake or hug. What will she think of me? What will I think of her? This is it. After a week of anticipation, after many visits to the dating site to re-visit the five photos that she has posted, after re-reading her profile to gather more insight, after re-playing the two-hour phone conversation in my mind and trying to recall her voice, her accent, her laughter, this is the moment of truth. The first few minutes can decide the next two hours.

I check in with myself. Gauge my desperation on a scale of one to ten. Figure it's about a six. I want this to work. After four years online, who wouldn't want something to work. I've begun to lose faith. It's tough at this age to find compatibility, most of us are set in our patterns, good enough on our own that we don't have to settle, yet yearn for a companion, a soulmate.

Ten minutes.

I keep my eyes on the door. Remembering the down escalator at Santa Barbara airport. Waiting for Suzanne. Attempting to climb the fence to gain access to English Rose; then there was Angelina, and then … I'm so damn tired of this game. What do I have to do to make it stop? "Love yourself. Stop looking for someone to rescue you. Become whole. Quiet the monkey mind." Yes, I know, I know, but I just can't seem to do it. Am I even ready to meet Kristan? What exactly am I offering? "Minor wounding. Held together by bandages. In need of repair. Character Reference: The Elder." Another sip of wine; make that a gulp as she walks through the door. I know it's her because she looks like her picture, only better. She dresses well, with a blue leather jacket and black leather pants. Smiles and walks straight towards me. I'm up, on my feet, arms extended. Done this so many times it's a reflex. A handshake that segues into a hug.

"Hi Kristan."

"Hello Richard."

"How was the drive?"

"Long, I've got to use the ladies' room," she says.

"It's right back there," I say, pointing toward the dimly lit corner of the restaurant.

I watch her walk. Confident, well-shaped, maybe a little heavy in the rear, stretching those leathers, but I like that. Extra padding, a perfect buffer for a man on the mend.

Dinner goes well. More wine. The rain is coming down in buckets and we're hoping it subsides before she begins her long journey back to Santa Ynez. Easy chatter, and enough trust that she agrees to a nightcap back at my house. Waiting out the rain. She follows the nearly new Infiniti in her very new Volvo SUV, which crosses the puddles and fallen branches like a sleek black tank, right behind me.

Home. I have enough firewood to start a blaze and pretty soon we are settled into the sofa like two old friends, listening to Gary Clark Jr. play his blues guitar and discussing the art of acupuncturing an aggressive Jack Russell. She has a couple of small scars on her fingers to attest to her learning curve. A glass of wine, a hit on the vapor pipe, and the rain is pelting down so I suggest she spends the night in the guest room. She thanks me for the offer but declines, saying she needs to be at her office by nine for an appointment with a depressed guinea pig.

Kristan looks very pretty in the light from the fire, but am I thinking about sex? Strangely, not at all. More about how nice it is to have a smart, good looking woman to share the warmth of a fire on a rainy night. Companionship; I get it, or I'm beginning to.

This could be a breakthrough, and worthy of discussion with the Elder.

At this point, and just before she leaves, she gets up to use the bathroom. While walking away she mentions that she needs to start exercising again because she's put on a little weight, particularly in her thighs and hips.

"I've got a fat ass," she says.

And at that point my self-diagnosed Tourette's nearly ends the evening.

"Yeah, you probably need to lose five or ten pounds."

She stops, turns and looks at me.

I smile like the idiot that I am. Even I, trainer of many bodies and prideful of my ability to make real and honest assessments of strength and bodyfat, understand that there are lines not to be crossed. Like agreeing with a woman when she tells you she has a fat ass. And to do that on a first date is really asking for trouble.

"I'm only kidding," I say, but she knows I wasn't.

Without answering, she walks to the bathroom, leaving me on the sofa feeling like I've been air smacked. She's smiling when she comes out; and I'm hopeful that the remark has been forgotten. We walk outside to her car.

"I really enjoyed meeting you," I say, holding her door open. Echoes of "fat ass" reverberate in time with the thunder from above. Why did I do it? Could it be the inner saboteur, waiting for things to go right so he can make them go wrong?

She turns and kisses me. It's a tight-lipped kiss, lasting only a few seconds, and feels rather hard and unforgiving, but it's something, an offering of peace after my insult and I'm grateful.

"Me too," she says. Hops in her car and drives off into the watery night.

*

I restrain myself an entire day before I text Kristan. During that time, aside from training a couple of clients and writing a few pages of a thriller that I delete within minutes of reading them, I think of Kristan. Up there in Santa Ynez, sticking needles into moody guinea pigs, fighting off a pack of aggressive Jack Russell terriers. Wondering if she'll ever see me again. Wishing I could have a re-do of that evening without the five-or-ten pounds remark. Did I destroy any hope of further contact? One way to find out.

Hi Kristan, it's Richard. Thinking of coming up your way this weekend, may I take you to dinner?

Nothing in return. Not for a day. Then two, and I'm in internet agony. I can't text again because that looks desperate. Wondering what she thinks of me, and whether that tight little kiss meant anything at all, other than a diversion to set up her escape. Paranoia runs deep.

Another day passes.

The problem with being a writer is time and imagination. When not involved in the process of creating something with words, when there is too much time to sit and think, and the mind is not focused on a particular story and transferring that story to the page, the imagination, the writer's gift, can become a terrible enemy. Creating wild scenarios, many unpleasant, and most exaggerated. The mind is a powerful instrument, and like a wild horse, must be controlled, reined in. But when it's on the loose and galloping, small things are often blown out of all proportion. Attempting to rein the horse in, the rational mind says, "Come on, I've met her once. I hardly know her. It was her fault. She brought her fat ass into the conversation. I was only being funny. It's her problem, not mine." This rationality is countered by, "I really offended her. She thinks I'm an asshole. She's ghosting me. Why can't I be more sensitive and keep my mouth shut?" Ghosted. Tossed out like a stained shirt. Accompanied by thoughts of her black Swedish tank, rolling down the long, lonely driveway on its way back to cowboy town, Kristan at the wheel with her panoramic smile, watching me grow smaller and smaller in the rearview mirror, until I disappear. Poof. Blip ... Ghosted.

By now it's Thursday.

Have I learned anything at all in the past four years? Why am I lying in my bed at eight o'clock, wondering if I am destined to walk, or, depending upon the severity of my arthritis, limp the final miles of my journey, alone. *Hoo-hoo* ... I hear that owl again, out there somewhere ... bringing back the echoes of Hank Williams and his soulful voice: *So lonesome I could cry.*

Another *hoo* from the perch and I enter into an inner philosophical discourse, thinking of everyone I know who is alone in bed this night, many, acknowledging that all of us are ultimately alone, all of us face and feel fear and are aware of death. All of us search for love. Unconditional love, the only real antidote to suffering. But how do we get there, into that state of love? I'm just like you. You are just like me. Even Kristan, the goddess from "Norvay," the one with the large derrière and the indestructible black tank, is searching for love.

Ping!

I look down at my cell phone. Below my last text, the one suggesting dinner in Santa Ynez, are the words, *Love to.*

Two words that change everything, and love is one of them; and it only took a week, an entire week, a week in which I fell prey to my own insecurities, my lack of faith, self-belief; a week in which I suffered.

Why?

Am I listening?

Am I leaning anything?

A rush of euphoria clouds any lessons the wise old owl may be trying to teach. The ego rises like a phoenix, back in the game. This time I won't blow it with a flippant remark. Another shot at the title, the good-looking babe on my arm. Another hundred and twenty miles on the odometer. Another brandishing of the gold card. Thank you, Amex, you'll buy me a partner yet.

More texting.

Kristan suggests the restaurant.

*

Clothes carefully selected. Hair trimmed. Infiniti washed, polished and vacuumed. Gas tank is full. Wallet is in my pocket. Gold card is in my wallet. Ready to go.

One last thing, I'm dog sitting Penny the Chihuahua, and she's coming to dinner because I can't leave her at home for fear she'll pee on the white sofa. It's cool; I've already checked, and the restaurant is dog friendly, as long as we are seated on the terrace. Perhaps a real plus in showing my gentle side. Besides, Kristan is an animal acupuncturist; she'll love Penny.

At times like these, because my need is great, I don't think about tomorrow. It doesn't matter what dinner costs. It doesn't matter that I'll be driving home at night and that the glare from oncoming headlights nearly blinds me. It doesn't matter that I don't really have a job and that money is finite. All that matters is that I get to Santa Ynez and see Kristan. Why is this so important?

Perhaps it's because I've had a partner for thirty-six years, if both marriages are counted, and I'm used to having someone around, someone to talk to, to exchange ideas with, to take on projects together, to bring me coffee while I'm writing, someone to take away that feeling that I am alone; it's that singular support system that I cannot seem to find on my own. Does that make me weak? Does that make everyone in a marriage, or a long-term relationship, weak, or lacking inner strength? I don't think so. So, why, at this age, am I having such trouble finding that relationship again?

"You're not ready," says the Elder.

Then how come I was ready before, twice, and how come neither lasted?

"Because you didn't work at it; neither of you communicated your needs, individuated, and surrendered the ego for the whole."

*

"Love to." Spurred on by those two words, with the low black Infiniti set in "Sport" mode, Penny nestled in my lap, watery brown eyes looking up at me as if to say, "Hey partner, slow down;" I downshift my way through the winding mountain pass, squealing around sharp bends, feeling like a twenty-year-old, on my way to cowboy town and a dinner with the Ice Maiden.

*

I arrive first. Get a quiet table on the outdoor patio, warmed by overhead heaters, and far enough from other diners that conversation can be intimate, and Penny will not attack. Tie her to the table leg, order a glass of Pinot Noir, the heart healthy preference for men traveling in "Sport" mode and anxiously awaiting the latest woman of his dreams. Even I, at this point, can see the futility of my actions. It's a repetitive cycle. Yet, I cannot seem to break it. How much pain is necessary to crack through the shell of understanding?

Lots.

The door opens and Kristan enters; she looks great, dressed beautifully in tight jeans with a touch of rock 'n roll in her zebra-painted calfskin boots. There's something expensive about her, and money is no object. Whatever she wants. Whatever she needs. An aperitif. Wine. Food. Courvoisier. Bring it on. The reward is holding hands across the table while eye-gazing and the promise of another date. Finally, it's time to go. Penny has been magnificent, quiet and reserved, nestling into my leg. I lift her up as Kristan, animal expert and needle artist, reaches out to stroke her.

The sound is like a chainsaw, but sharper and nastier, as Penny, my jealous bed partner, attaches herself to Kristan's middle finger. I pull back. Penny doesn't let go. Pull again. It's a tug of war and Kristan's finger is the rope. More snarling, a shout from me that turns heads, "Penny! Stop it!!" Until, finally, the Chihuahua scorned retires to a submissive position beneath my right armpit.

"I'm sorry, really sorry," I say.

Kristan extends her hand; there's an imprint of tiny teeth but, miraculously, no blood.

"Typical Chihuahua," she says. "Probably jealous."

That annoys me... Penny is far from "typical", having rescued me from nocturnal misery more than once. Providing a warm, albeit tiny, body to cuddle with in the night. Besides, Kristan is supposed to be the master-of-animals. Don't blame Penny. And ... don't feel so special, she bites everyone.

With Chihuahua constrained beneath my arm, we walk to the black tank and say goodnight. I bend for a kiss and receive something dry, hard and tight; it's like trying to suck a cork from a Champagne bottle.

Headed home. A man and his part-time dog. We understand each other. Alone, together. My best relationship in years.

Driving cautiously, in automatic this time, my saber-toothed guardian sleeping blissfully in my lap. Through the mountains, taking curves very carefully, feeling emotionally flattened, recalling the kiss of the cork, a far cry from the fearless matador of three hours ago.

A text from Kristan heralds my arrival in the long, ever-changing driveway.

That was a beautiful second date. I hope to see you again, soon. Bring Penny.

My God!

I text back, *I adore you.*

There's hope in Norway, the ice is melting. Thanks, Penny. We did it.

*

Another evening at the same restaurant, this time without Penny, who has rejoined Ingrid's pack of Chihuahuas on the other side of town, taking on all comers, regardless of breed or size, and darting out from beneath chairs and sofas, like an electric eel, to bite feet and ankles…anything that moves.

Kristan is far less passionate. Still the Ice Maiden, slow to respond to my texts, which I am informed, by experienced friends and an article I've googled, is a sure sign that she's not all that interested in me. Tough to accept, and slightly contradicted by the fact that we're here, on the terrace, beneath the patio heater, with accordion musettes from Provence playing softly from the overhead speakers. Sipping rosé and speaking in hushed tones. I attempt to make forays into her past life, open her up, get her to talk about herself.

"What was your last relationship like?"

She looks at me. Hesitating, as if I'm encroaching and, perhaps, trying to enter private places.

"I'm just curious," I add.

She sits back in her chair.

"He was a very successful lawyer," she says. "Made lots of money and drove a Tesla. I loved driving that car. It was so fast."

Tesla? The car I wanted but could not afford. Maybe I can't afford the Ice Maiden, either. Financially, emotionally, the thoughts cross my mind.

"Why did it end?" I ask.

"When he worked, I hardly saw him, but when he was around, he didn't give me enough space."

Space? A word I hear often while navigating the waters of romance after fifty. Everyone wants their space. Personal space. Creative space. Inner space. Outer space. Any kind of space.

And time. Time can be a killer; too little and the relationship suffers from lack of attention, too much togetherness and claustrophobia can set in, followed by suffocation. Keeping it healthy requires balance, and a great deal of self-knowledge and honesty.

"What are you looking for?" I ask.

Her answer is cryptic. "I'll know when I find it."

The dinner ends, the Gold Card is extended and received, another hundred and forty dollars added to the balance, and we walk from the restaurant to the parking lot. Another moment of truth. Is this the night that the Ice Maiden melts, her lips softening, perhaps parting as our tongues entwine in that delicate dance of courtship?

Straight to the black tank. With a bleep from her remote the door opens; she turns to face me. I manage a shy smile, vulnerable, but at ease, arms extended, hands upon her shoulders, drawing her body gently into a loving but tentative embrace, lips merging and … Jesus … it's worse than the champagne cork. Now I've got the corkscrew, a mouth pursed so tight it feels pointed. The alpha male rears his head, as I force my tongue forward in an effort to penetrate the wall of pink flesh and muscle separating me from the Ice Maiden's heart.

I want in.

She spits me out.

Visions of English Rose and her anaconda tongue, except, this time, it's my tongue and I'm the Rose. Standing there. Embarrassed. Frustrated.

Then, as if she didn't notice my attempt at forced entry, she says, "Thank you for a lovely third date."

I can't believe it: she's counting. One, two, three, and maybe I get kissed on the fourth. Is this how they do it in "Norvay?" The mouth opening like an aperture; the width and length informed by the amount of dates, money and time spent together, space given, personal and otherwise, and, perhaps, cars driven. A Tesla may enter the aperture on the second date, while an Infiniti, particularly a pre-owned model, may have to go a full five, even six to get inside.

"Thank you," I reply. The ego adds, "May I see you again?"

Obviously, a glutton for punishment, sure that when I crack this safe there will be gold inside. True love, real commitment, eroticism, lacy bras, fishnet stockings, thongs by Victoria's Secret, forbidden Scandinavian sexual practices. Maybe a pair of lederhosen. And, companionship, of course.

"Call me," she suggests. Sounds like she means it.

"I will."

On the slow walk to my car, which now, ironically, is parked beside a red Tesla, I envision the Elder, the list on his lap, Bic ballpoint in hand, asking if Kristan's name is spelled with an *e* or an *a.*

I really don't want to do this anymore.

*

"Call me," she said.

And three days later, I do.

"Hello, Kristan."

"Hello, Richard."

"How would you like to spend a day with me this weekend? I was thinking of Butterfly Beach in Montecito? And there's a great little French restaurant ..."

"I can't."

"Oh ... I'm sorry."

"I've got shooting pains down my right side. From my lower back, all the way to my right thigh. Maybe sciatica."

"Have you seen a chiropractor?"

"Yes, but it still hurts."

"I'm really sorry. Maybe when you feel better we could ..."

Her voice is abrupt. "I'm not sure when that will be, the pain is going from my back, all the way down through my hip ..."

She hesitates and I feel the empty space.

It's coming. The subconscious Tourette's monster, charging up the steps to crash through the door. Taking over. Doing what I need to but can't. The part of me that doesn't want to do this anymore. The finisher. Delivered with a flourish, a dash of good humor, but delivered.

"You mean, all the way down through your fat ass?"

Silence, as my words hang there in space, like rotting fruit, ready to fall from the branch.

"What did you just say?

I cower and attempt a cover-up.

"I said, I'm sorry you can't make it this weekend. I really am."

"Did you just say I have a fat ass?"

"Come on, Kristan, you know I was kidding."
"But you said it, didn't you?"
"Yes."
"I'm letting you go."
Click …

*

The Elder studies me with a mixture of disappointment and compassion.

"You probably set this up to fail," he says.

"Because of the corkscrew kisses?" I ask.

"I believe that was an indication of her unwillingness to open up to you or be honest. You sensed it. It's a subconscious signal. You knew the relationship wasn't going to work, but, still, you wanted it so badly, willing to sacrifice your true self, that your subconscious, that unquestioning servant, had to step in." He looks down at the list, resting like a cat in his lap. Adding, "In time, you will develop a deeper sense of awareness. More honesty. More self-esteem. You deserve more than a corkscrew." He lifts the Bic, like a lethal weapon, primed for the execution. It hovers above the page.

"Is Kristan spelled with an *a* or an *e*?"

***

~14~

The episode with Kristan is sobering, forcing me to take a good look at my values, the way I spend my time, and where I place my priorities. Finding a partner, whether the Elder deems me ready or not, has become my full-time job; I'm on the dating sites first thing in the morning and last thing at night, with several stops in between. What began, at least for me, as a side event, a novelty, something I did because I was told that everyone else was doing it, has become my main object of attention, an addiction, costing time, money and self-esteem.

My stress levels are high. It's an accumulation of things, not the least of which is living alone, lack of sound sleep, dwindling finances, and this pursuit of a magical other who will, somehow, make everything all right, even though, somewhere deep down, I understand the utter fantasy of the magical other. There is no rescue from another, although I'll settle for a life raft, just to keep me afloat while I hail an ocean liner to carry me back to port. But the straw that finally breaks the old Romeo's back is about to land.

*

Seated at my computer, pondering writing projects and fighting a desire to scour the sites for new faces and send out another cry for companionship, like a message in a bottle, the phone rings.

It's my ex ... "Hi, it's me. Sorry to have to tell you this."

Her voice is anxious, and my immediate thoughts are of the boys, has something happened?

"What is it?"

"Get ready," she says. As she speaks, I notice a small maroon sedan ambling up the driveway. "You are about to be served."

"I'll call you back," I reply as the Kia stops in front of the house and the driver, a short man in slacks, highly polished black shoes, a striped shirt and a wide blue tie alights. He's carrying a big white envelope in his hand and walks to my front door as I open it.

"Richard La Plante?"

"Yes."

He extends the hand bearing the envelope. His face looks pained; I'm not sure if he actually feels this or if it's an act, something he's perfected over the years to avoid being punched in the mouth.

"Sorry … but you've been served," he says.

By whom? For what?

He hands me a pen and produces another legal pad, then indicates a place to put my signature, right below my ex-wife's.

It's all over quickly and the Kia's gone, with me left holding the bag, in this case the envelope.

I open it. Read the first paragraph, under Plaintiff.

My entire body goes icy cold. No hyperbole here; this a real, physical feeling, as if someone or something has just pulled the plug on my blood supply. I'm numb, head to toes. Have to sit down. The plaintiff is my ex-neighbor, an eccentric multimillionaire who loves to litigate, everything from trashcan placement to the amount of times each person used the electric gate and how the bill was divided. Litigation is his passion, his reason-to-be, mostly petty stuff, but this is not petty. This suit is claiming fraud, property theft, misrepresentation and a stack of offenses that I can't take in, not in one sitting, but the crux of it is that we sold the house without a grant of right of easement over a patch of land that he owns, or claims he does. We did not get his consent. Our house sale is illegal.

I call our lawyer.

He says not to panic. Wait till he phones and speaks to the buyers.

The lawyer gets back to me.

The news is not good. The litigating lunatic does, in fact, own the patch of land and has blocked access to the driveway with a line of boulders, transported by back-hoe, driven by himself, wearing Army combat fatigues and an LA Dodgers cap. The new owners watched from the sidelines, and now, after several years, no longer have access to their property, or, legally, perhaps, his property. They are threatening to injunct all our assets and freeze our bank accounts until the matter is resolved, or we give them their money back. Claiming we did not disclose the easement issue, an issue that we had no idea existed.

"This could end up in court," my friend, the lawyer says.

"Court?"

"Yes, with a jury trial."

I celebrate this news with two gourds of mate, a highly caffeinated Argentinian tea, and a ferocious workout in the gym, including an intense three-minute bare-handed round on my heavy bag, which includes bellowing my neighbor's name as I demolish the hundred-pound sack of sand with bleeding knuckles.

My heart is tripping like a jackhammer. Jury trial? Years of pain, torture, aloneness and fear surge through my body and into my fists.

I want to kill.

But who am I killing? My neighbor? The new buyers? My ex-wife? Myself?

Doesn't matter.

The heavy bag wins.

My heartrate hits 166 and stays there. Back to the house. Lie down on the bed. Put on the blood pressure cuff. Still 166. Twenty-minutes later and it's not going down. Something's wrong. Try not to panic. No need to panic, your heart is doing it for you.

Into the car. Make the ten-minute drive to the hospital. Into the ER.

"It's my heart. It's pounding and won't stop."

"Come this way."

Secured in a cot-bed and connected to several machines by a web of wires as my blood pressure soars and my heart continues to beat to its own frenetic rhythm, and completely out of time.

My bed is tucked inside a curtained cubicle, out of eyesight but within earshot of a man who sounds like he is dying. Moans and groans and the occasional shout for help.

The ER doctor arrives and sits in a chair beside me. He looks to be in his fifties, with thinning brown hair and sharp brown eyes, eyes that have been to war more than once.

"When do I get out of here?" I ask.

Another shout from the bed next door, a few more groans, and a long, low sigh. Perhaps a sign that a kindly nurse has administered a massive dose of sedation.

"Is there something you need to tell me?" the ER doctor asks.

I find this whole thing depressing, and frightening. Remembering my mini-stroke, or pinched artery, and wondering if it's all connected.

Still, I try for a touch of bravado.

"Yes, I'd like to leave."

He does not share my sense of irony; in fact, he seems annoyed.

He stares at me; I stare back. Finally, he speaks.

"All right, I'll get straight to the point, how much do you drink?"

His eyes penetrate mine, as if he knows my darkest secret and is demanding a confession. Either that or I must join the man in the nearby cubicle and submit to medical experiments, clinical trials and deep sedation.

"How much?" he demands.

"One glass of wine at night," I answer.

His eyes narrow, growing more intense; I sense that he doesn't believe me. Is this man a doctor or a professional interrogator?

"Sometimes two," I say, beginning to sound like a sleep-deprived prisoner in the first throes of spilling the beans. A long, contented sigh from the man in the nearby cubicle and I'm made aware of the blessed relief that is promised if I fully comply.

Here it comes. "Every now and then, half a bottle."

"Half a bottle?" he repeats, turning my answer into a question. It's a technique the Elder uses on occasion, to extract buried emotions or force elaboration on a particular issue.

"Yes."

"Never an entire bottle?"

Silence, as the prisoner clams up.

Another contented groan from the cot next door, then something that sounds like a long, slow flatulent release, testifying to the wonder of pharmaceuticals.

"Look, I'm trying to help you," the doctor continues. "A lot of times an irregular heartbeat, is caused by binge drinking. I see it all the time in here, but it's mostly younger people. Are you under a lot of stress?"

"Yes, I am," I answer, sparing him the indulgent details of staring at a long dark driveway and listening to that lonesome whippoorwill, or in my case an owl.

Suddenly, the sharp eyes soften and the man in the white lab coat looks very tired and very human.

"Okay … I had a bottle of wine last night, on my own," I continue, "and then started the morning with a lot of caffeine before I went to the gym."

He smiles; it's a kind smile.

"Do you think you can go five days without drinking?"

I get it. He thinks I'm an alcoholic.

"Yes, I can go five days."

"Okay. You do that. And I'm going to send you to a cardiologist."

Cardiologist? This sounds serious.

"Do I really need a cardiologist?"

"I want you to have a stress test," he confirms.

*

I last ten days without wine and twelve minutes on the treadmill, which is continually adjusted to create a steeper angle, until my heart has reached a maximum rate and I'm sucking for air, then I'm laid, gasping like a trout on the chopping board, upon a narrow table and echo scanned, which is an ultra-sound of my heart.

A week later, I'm wearing a monitor strapped around my chest and encouraged to carry on with all my usual activities, which include my high intensity gym workouts and sex, as if that may actually be a feature of my current existence.

Every time I do a pull-up, or a bar dip I wonder if this it, the big one, the last rep, where I actually go to maximum failure, as in a major coronary. Only to be found by one of my sons. "At least the old man went out doing what he loved to do," they say at the wake. "I wonder how many reps he got before it happened?" Although since they are both in college, hundreds of miles away, I may be slightly mummified by the time they discover me. Or hanging by the gymnastic rings in a state of calcification.

My imagination runs wild.

The monitor is surrendered, and I am diagnosed with AFib, an irregular heartbeat, and a moderately leaky mitral valve, which one doctor suggests I may want to have repaired within the next year. I'm not sure what "repair" means but I imagine the worst. I often imagine the worst. Laid on a table, intubated. On a ventilator. Opened up. Broken heart removed from body. Ex-wife extracted. Stitched back up. The Zipper. No one to take care of me.

My writer's imagination slips into overdrive.

I don't sleep for seven nights. Lying there, in the darkness. No woman. No whippoorwill. No love. No hope. Not even the owl… Alone, more than I have ever felt in my life.

I am going to die. Yes, but I already knew that. Everyone knows that. No, not quite. It's just a possibility, with a buffer of years between probability and certainty. At fifty, there's always thirty or more years to go, thirty wonderful years, full of hope and promise, at sixty, there's still plenty left, and the time ahead is often better than the time at hand, more hope, more promise. But at seventy-two with a broken heart, now that's a different story. Exhausted. Feeling sorry for myself, an old man, abandoned by his younger wife. A man who always relied upon his charm, his health, his physicality and his strength. Where is it now?

Real strength?

Then comes the darkest night of my life. Sleep won't take me. But the waking nightmares do. Right down the stairs to the basement, where all the shadows lay in wait. Ready to eat me alive, cracking through that shell of the ego, breaking it wide open, with hammers and pickaxes, finally and irrevocably. Take a look inside.

I don't want to, but I'm compelled: I see pride, arrogance, that feeling of being special, chosen, as if the world owes me something; but knowing, at the same time, that I am not special, and the world owes me nothing. We are all the same, living and dying, with a brief dance in between.

I look up. My ceiling has exposed rafters; I had them painted white when I renovated the house. Would one of those white beams be strong enough to hold my body, tied with the sash from my Japanese kimono, the robe that is decorated with cherry blossoms, a symbol of impermanence?

I keep staring, imagining myself, sash wrapped round my neck, hanging from that rafter.

All alone. I'm so tired. So scared. Everything is closing in on me. My body is breaking. My mind is breaking. Moonlight through the window, shadows from the trees. I don't control any of it. I don't control anything. My heart beating its crazy beat. Say a prayer. No one is listening. Help me, Dad. Help me, Mom. There's no one there. Can't get out of this place. This place of being alone.

Get up. Out of bed. Away from the rafter. Don't look up. Don't look back. Pick up the phone. Call a friend, Ingrid. I trust her. She trusts me.

"I think I'm losing it," I say.

We are used to joking but she knows this is not a joke.

"Breathe," she answers. "Do what you teach. Breathe, long slow breaths."

I breathe, one time, two times, three. Long and slow. Say thank you to my friend and put the phone down. Inhale. Exhale. The panic ebbs. The urgency decreases. Keep breathing. My mind begins to change. I really am okay. In the here and now, I'm just fine. Moonlight. Shadows. It's a beautiful night.

Suicide. I understand. When everything is in the rearview mirror and there's nothing ahead, except suffering, and being alone, forever. All paths lead to the ledge and there is no way out, except over.

I get it.

I really get it.

Surrender. Let go.

Breathe till the morning light. Take a shower. Wash the film of fear from the skin. Meditate. Visit the Elder.

"You've got the same heart you had the last time you saw me," he says. "Nothing has changed. You may have had that leak for twenty years. AFib is common. Your body has aged. Everyone's body ages. Parts wear out. You're still alive. You're healthy. You've got so much left. No one knows what's around the bend. All we have is now. This is it. Your chance to be who you really are. Authentic."

"I'm seventy-two years old. Am I still giving birth to myself?" I ask.

"Yes, you are, with the help of some induced labor. And, maybe, you should have a bit of compassion for yourself."

*

Then, with the further help of some prescription Ativan to relieve anxiety, and an overnight with Penny to remind me what unconditional love feels like, I get some sleep. After that, I get a job.

Writing a one-man show for an outlaw, or an ex-outlaw, the longest serving president of the Hells Angels Motorcycle Club, now retired, or "out bad," as described by his former club, which means excommunicated for reasons I will never know, but George has already starred in a hit TV show and this assignment is a Godsend for me, since I can't come up with a new idea of my own and, being an ex-Harley rider, outlaw culture has always held a fascination.

It also means a little money.

George arrives daily at 11 AM, not on a '57 Panhead or a road-worn Electra Glide but driving a pale blue Nissan Cube, which looks about as tall as it is long. He's covered in wall-to-wall tattoos, attired in black trainers, high black socks, long black shorts, the kind that fall below the knees, and a black T-shirt, a seventy-year-old gangbanger after my own leaking heart. Packing two concealed knives which he brandishes, upon my request, to display skills honed by years of instruction and drills. Arms whipping in circles, he presents an impenetrable razor-edged fortress. He's funny, fearless and charismatic; it's James Cagney on steroids. "Made it, Ma. Top of the world." Let me take you for a spin around the block in my Cube.

He talks.

I listen.

He leaves at five.

I write.

I'm inspired. Feeling like I've had a double dose of testosterone, or maybe it's a set of borrowed balls, or pumped ego, but I don't need the Ativan because I'm writing all night, then sleeping. Screw the heart, screw the arthritis, screw the age, I'm in the club and George is president.

Telling me stories of the road; riding from San Francisco to LA, soaring on a megadose of Owsley acid at a hundred miles an hour. In the wind. Fights with their rival club, the Outlaws. Hanging with Mickey Rourke, getting stoned with David Carradine. He's mesmerizing, spouting tales of ol' ladies, bikers' girlfriends, and what it means to be a house mouse, a female hanger on. Tells me he envies my freedom, my home and my ability to attract various women of various ages. Likes the way I play the guitar; reminds him of Steven Stills. Tells me things he claims no one else knows, no one else has ever heard. Secrets of his past. I believe him, most of the time, the other times don't matter; I'm feeling good, like I want to climb on my old Harley Springer and head out on the highway. Forgetting the past few years, forgetting the cherry blossom sash and the snow-white rafter above my bed. Whatever I've been through, George has been through worse, including prison time and solitary confinement. He's lost everything but he's coming back. Stronger than ever. Give me my cut-offs and my outlaw patch, I've got a new brother; I'm in the club.

*

My newly resurrected machismo extends to the dating sites, except this time it is different. I am different, changing gradually, but changing. And look what it's taken so far: illness, loss, fear, enormous amounts of fear, a walk to the edge and a quick look into the abyss, coupled with acceptance and a touch of letting go. People talk about change, say they've changed, then revert to every old pattern they've had since childhood when the pressure hits. It takes lots to change. Maybe even hitting rock bottom, and the will to keep going when there seems nowhere left to go.

But here I am.

With fear as my prime motivator.

But love, where is love?

More dates from the site, mostly coffee or a glass of wine at a local winery; I'm getting more honest with this stuff. I meet a police officer, an undertaker, a florist, a doctor, all the while beginning to understand what I need and not projecting my needs onto the person sitting across from me, with needs of their own. The desperation is fading. Replaced by a sense of what I want. These dates almost never extend to a follow-up and it is usually me who knows when it will not work; I say it first, then move on. Home to my bed, with the snow-white rafter above.

George and I finally have a script for the one-man show and, after a meeting with the producer, it is decided that I should direct it. I am not a director, have never directed anything beyond a bar dip in the gym and say as much, protesting, but am coerced by promises of cross-country tours and custom T-shirts, selling by the thousands.

The show is titled *Outlaw*.

Most days, and after the real outlaw departs and the Cube, carrying the man in black, makes its snail-like exit from my long driveway, the outlaw-director relaxes by going online and looking at faces in search of a female of interest. So many faces, so many of us out there, so many stories.

Then, one evening, following a living room rehearsal in which George speaks tenderly of the son he lost to a diabetic coma, which moves me towards introspection, thoughts of my two sons, and reminds me of the brevity of all our lives, I sit down at the computer and see someone new. Her screen name is Emerald, and she has long dark hair, honey-brown eyes, an embroidered Mexican blouse and a silver chain bearing a cross, ethnic but chic. Her smile is warm. Her profession is given as chef and her profile is short. "Looking for an authentic man to spend some real time with." Authentic, did she actually write authentic? Authentic, that's my middle name. I message her with a sense of purpose. "Hello Emerald, I may be just what you are looking for. Working daily on my authenticity. Getting there but could use the help of a real woman." I press send then have immediate doubts about my authenticity. Did I just sound glib, maybe a poser? Did I just show disrespect for her request for something real? It's too late to take the message back and I cannot message her again with some feeble excuse, because that would reek of insecurity. No, I've done it, now I have to stand by my words.

I get email notification first thing in the morning. Her message reads, *My real name is Josey and I like voices. May I hear yours?*

I like voices, too; I understand, there's so much in the vibration of the voice. "Sure, Josey," I reply, "let's talk tonight, how about 8 o'clock?" And I give her my cell phone number.

During rehearsal and realizing that my authenticity is on the line, as I am about to be judged by my vocal tones, I pick up my guitar and sing a song I've written for *Outlaw*, loosening up the voice box in preparation for the big call.

George listens, then tells me I sound like Bob Dylan, who he's met backstage. Bob Dylan, now there's authenticity. This comparison does great things for my confidence. I'm actually not sure if George means everything he says, any more than I'm certain that he's told me secrets that no other living soul knows, but I am in the club, and I'm riding.

All the way till 8 o'clock when the phone rings.

"Hello, this is Josey." Her voice is low and silky, very sexy.

Bob Dylan replies.

"Hello Josey."

We talk for a few minutes. I learn that she lives in Goleta, about forty miles away, and works in a high-end restaurant in Santa Barbara, which raises immediate concerns of the Asian cop and the possibility of running into Angelina and being strangled by a bright red thong. Still, it's all going well, till Josey pauses.

"May I ask you a question?"

"Of course, anything at all." I answer.

There's another short pause, then the silky voice whispers, "How big is your penis?"

This is a first, and I'm not sure how to handle it. Wish George was here. This must have happened to him in his riding days. He'd have an answer, but he's not here. I'm on my own, just me and my penis.

I pause. Considering. Should I say "10 inches" and achieve porn star status by phone, or keep it authentic, which is a lot less exciting but saves that moment of embarrassing truth if we ever actually meet and get naked.

One of the Four Agreements cross my mind. "Be impeccable with your words." Lies have consequences.

"I guess I'm about average," I say, although it sounds a bit weak. Who wants to be "about average," in anything?

"So, it's not big?"

Josey is not giving up. More detail required.

"Maybe six inches," I answer, "but I used to be five feet nine and a half and now, I've shrunk, I'm only five-eight and a half. I'm not sure how big my penis is these days. Guess it all depends on blood flow."

Now, it's her turn to be quiet. Did I make the grade, or fail? Left to buy penis enlargement pills from Ron Jeremy's infomercial site or maybe a penis pump. Is 8 inches her cut-off number? Will she request photos, with a ruler placed against the protesting member? Proof of life?

About to kiss the night goodbye when she says.

"May I come see you?"

Accepted, in all my averageness, a man and his organ, at one, at peace.

"Yes, I'd love that," I answer.

It's been a while, but I feel a vibration in my root chakra as I place down the phone. Telling myself, there will be no romance this time, no heartache, no insecurity, no waiting by the cell phone for a one-line message that can be interpreted in a thousand different ways, "she loves me, she loves me not," or an emoji of a heart, or a kiss, or two hands in prayer.

No, I'm going to be selfish. Respectful, but selfish. Get what I need and keep my heart out of the exchange. The Elder may not approve but my new mentor, George, will applaud.

I am an ... Outlaw ...

***

~15~

Rehearsals continue in my living room. George is a natural; he loves being in the spotlight, proven by the fact that he once ran a leg of the Olympic torch relay, after hustling his way into the games by making a five-thousand-dollar donation in the name of HAMC, the club initials, but misinterpreted by the Olympic committee as a legitimate and law-abiding corporation. It made the news, and George was, way back then, a star. Biker runs, biker parties and biker women; I figure he's just the man to advise me regarding my upcoming meeting with Josey.

"Just hang loose and see what she wants," he says, after I give him a run-down. "Doesn't sound like you're going to marry her. Big dick? Who the hell cares about having a big dick?" Following which he returns to his Cube and putters out of my driveway.

Things on the legal front are heating up. The police have enforced a removal of the boulders blocking access to the dream house and the litigator has countered by locking the electric gate. Forced to unlock it by the fire department, he's fuming. Word is, transferred by way of our lawyer, that the litigator wants to go to court, wants a jury trial. Wants to run with the Olympic torch.

Stress, why do we find it necessary to create stress? Maybe, because it makes us feel alive, before it kills us.

More stress as the producer of *Outlaw* issues dire warnings that George has never been on a stage in his life and we are not properly rehearsing. Claiming that *Outlaw* will be a disaster if we don't find a stage.

The man in black huffs, puffs, and exits by Cube.

I rent the theater of a local preparatory school.

We get in two rehearsals, under the lights, before the school runs a criminal background check through the police department on who is using their facilities and bars us from further theatrics, although by then, the producer has seen a live rehearsal and declares that we have a "hit" on our hands. Proposing an extensive tour, all the way to New York and off-Broadway, including the sale of hundreds of thousands of T-shirts. Perhaps a signature Cube.

And finally, it's Josey's turn to perform.

Rolling into my driveway in a four-door Hummer; the H2 is snow-white, reminiscent of the rafter in my bedroom, and I watch anxiously from the window, waiting for her to disembark and begin an assault on the house, wondering if she'll demand a complete inspection of my penis before she'll come inside. I feel shrinkage. This could be humiliating. George? I need some biker wisdom. "Big dick? Who the hell cares?" Thank you.

I stare at the Hummer, aglow in the afternoon sun. The door opens, and finally, she appears, climbing down from the driver's side, using the running board to assist her descent. Walking round the back of the big squared cage. Wavy hair and an attractive face, a little bit of the Barbie doll in the nose and lips, not dissimilar to her pictures, maybe a shade more cosmetic. Wearing a white tank top and tight, floral printed leggings. Looks like she has a good strong body; walking in long strides, like she means business. Hold on. What is she wearing on her feet? Big brown floppy things, like boats; maybe she needs them to operate the Hummer. The shoes don't quite go with the rest of her outfit, but, as George says, who the hell cares?

I open the door.

She kicks off the offending footwear and enters.

A moment of hesitation.

I extend a hand.

"How do you do, Josey?"

No hesitation on her part.

She bends forward and kisses me on the lips. It's a big, full warm kiss from big, full warm lips, with minimal tongue. Aggressively tasteful.

I've already told myself that this will not be a love affair; I've tried and failed with that. No, this will be a physical relationship. Nothing more. Now that I have a day job, with less time to sit around and visualize dying old and alone, I feel capable of something other than looking for the next great love of my life. I've heard it called "friends with benefits," and that is what I'm after. At least, that is what I tell myself I'm after. My new outlook and philosophy have become a mixture of Biker George and the Tribal Elder. A blend of road warrior and compassionate shrink, interchangeable according to my frame of mind.

*

We sit on the sofa and I offer a glass of wine, make light conversation about her work as a chef and listen attentively to what it takes to create a good saffron risotto. Following which I stand and perform several exercises with my breathing stick, a polished pole, that I use for breath training and conscious movement, moving it up and down and sideways to guide the inhales and exhalations. This seems to arouse her in ways that the risotto did not, and I contemplate segueing into some guitar playing perhaps to add a touch of yin to my yang physicality when she says, "I don't think we should fuck on our first date."

She's straightforward, that's for sure, very direct, and I appreciate it. It's no wonder she drives a Hummer and wears waterboards for shoes. I also notice that she keeps her cell phone handy, maybe to check for any other average-sized males.

"That's fine with me," I answer, slightly challenged. Is she presuming that there will be more dates? Then I recall the Ice Maiden, with her tight lips, Volvo SUV and the six dates to an open-mouth mandate; and vow, in an effort to love myself, not to fall prey to future ultimatums.

"But we can fool around," she adds, just as I head for another glass of wine and remember I have an upcoming appointment with the cardiologist, in the same week that my ex-wife and I sit down with the property lawyer to discuss our pending court trial.

Stress relief.

Well ... I wanted it. Now it's been offered. But can I handle it?

Sure, you can... Outlaw.

*

"Where's your bedroom?" she asks.

I point to a doorway behind the sofa, which leads to a set of narrow, winding stairs.

"Shall I lead the way?" she suggests.

I suffer a touch of nerves. Josey is the most straight-up, downright aggressive woman I have ever met. I'm feeling withdrawn. Shy. Suppose this is how a woman feels when a man gets pushy. Like, hold on, shouldn't we talk some more, get to know each other, have another six dates before we kiss?

"Have you been checked out lately?"

I'm not certain what she means. I hesitate.

"For STDs," she adds.

"I'm fine," I say. "Just had my physical." Which included bloodwork. I guess that would also include sexually transmitted diseases, but maybe not.

"Let's go," she says, picking up her cell phone. Then looking at me, "Sorry about this. I'm taking care of my mother and she sometimes gets very anxious when I leave her alone, so she texts me a lot."

"Is she sick?" I ask.

"Early onset dementia," she answers. "She gets confused and does some pretty strange things sometimes. I keep an eye on her."

This single thing, the fact that she's looking after her mother, eases me. Josey is human, not some predator. She's just short on time, like the rest of us. And, unlike some of the rest of us, she seems to know exactly what she wants, which is exactly what I've been telling myself that I want, a friend with benefits.

"Come on up," I say and walk to the stairway.

Josey follows my ascent, placing her cell phone on the night table and standing at the foot of my bed while I kick off my flip-flops and lie down, in my clothes, ready for more conversation, maybe some kissing, and whatever else "fooling around" entails. Not Josey. Bathed in the light of a setting sun cascading through open blinds, she begins to undress. The tank top is first, leaving a delicate pink bra, then come the leggings, leaving pale pink laced shorts. Her body is well-shaped, with sinewy arms and beautiful shoulders. Josey is sixty-two, and I'm glad of that. I don't need the projection of a young body to bolster my perception of myself, not anymore, not after the snow-white rafter, emergency rooms, cardiologists, lawsuits, sessions with the Elder and afternoons with George. I need real, and I'm getting it.

She looks at me as if to say, "Your turn."

It's like a game of strip poker, not that I've ever actually played.

I figure my white T-shirt is the thing I can most afford to lose, so off it comes. Then I unbutton the top button of my jeans to make sure my belly doesn't spill over. Vanity? Yes, still some of that. Seventy-two, but wants to look fifty. Not in this light, no chance.

Josey unhitches her bra and throws it on the bench by the bed. Small breasts, but real ones, and pretty. There's something primitive about this dance; it's been going on since the Garden of Eden, but every time is different, and every time is new.

Take off my jeans. Toss them to the floor. Got my black Calvin Kleins on with the button front. Still feeling safe.

Down come the laced shorts, kicked aside, and Josey is naked, all shaved and pink and friendly. She turns around and touches her toes, looking at me from the space between her legs. Holding the position.

My move.

She stands and turns back so she's facing me again, smiling. Hope that smile doesn't turn into a laugh 'cause here I go, removing the button-fronted Calvin Kleins. I'm excited, so it's not a shrunken disaster. In fact, looking down, it's a respectable showing, for an average Joe.

Josey gives me the once over, then her eyes settle on the area of interest in our initial phone call.

I feel like I'm auditioning for the leading role in a blockbuster, or at least an adult movie.

How long can her eyes linger? What's she thinking?

I look down to see how we're holding up. Please, don't die on me now.

She moves towards the bed.

"Perfect," she says.

*

The reason she finds me so sexually compatible is her ex-husband, who, she tells me, worked his way through university by performing in live sex shows in San Francisco. Now he's a marine biologist, but still possesses the instrument that facilitated his education. And, she says, sex was always painful, and got progressively worse; in fact, so painful that it was a contributing factor to their marriage break-up. She actually developed a phobia about it, which is the reason she vets all on-liners before meeting. I wonder how others have responded. Doesn't matter, because I seem to be the chosen one, at least by Josey.

So, I've got what I wanted, or thought I wanted, a friend with benefits.

*

One week later ...

If the back of the Chevrolet Volt was tight, the Infiniti is a broom closet, but still, after a dinner at a Japanese restaurant and several cups of sake, yes, blame it on the fermented rice, I find myself holed up with Josey on a suburban street in Santa Barbara lined with houses and used by several dog walkers. We are naked in the back of the Infiniti, our privacy insured by windows so steamed up that there's no view in, or out, so I can only wonder what's happening whenever I hear voices or footsteps.

The reason we cannot go to Josey's place is her mother, who, according to Josey, has become increasingly concerned as to who she is seeing and the time she spends away from home. So, gentleman that I am, I submit to being straddled in the back of my tight leather cubicle.

This type of lovemaking is awkward, particularly when the chance of discovery, even an arrest for lewd conduct, is a possibility. I believe this turns Josey on, and God help us if the Asian cop is working the night shift. I can imagine us, stark naked, being bent over the hood of the Infiniti as he applies a dose of pepper spray to my groin before cuffing us and hauling us away to the geriatric wing of the town lock-up. No, I can't do this.

"Sorry, Josey."

She dismounts slowly and tries to get her pants back on, kneeing me in the face by accident. Giving me a bloody nose which I plug with a torn piece of napkin from the sake supplier. Then it's my turn to dress, but due to various aches and pains I'm having a hard time getting back into my favored Calvin Kleins, and when I do, I place the left foot through the right leg then the right foot through the left and pull them up so I'm wearing them backwards. Off they come again. Seriously considering driving home naked before suggesting that Josey climb into the front seat, giving me more room to maneuver. Because of my nudity, I don't want to open the door of the car, so various gymnastic practices must be employed; remembering that it was only half an hour ago that, fueled by multiple cups of sake, I moved with the grace of a jungle cat in heat. Now, with my nose leaking blood and my jeans caught around my ankles, I feel like a decrepit bull elephant in a very tight cage. Luckily, Josey is athletic and manages the climb through the gap between seats with only a few groans. Allowing me room to spread out lengthwise across the narrow space, and pull my jeans up, then fumble my way back into my socks and shoes.

Mission accomplished, I open the rear door of the car, step out into the street, nod a cordial hello to a curious dog walker, re-enter through the driver's side door, start the engine and speed away. We're both laughing like a couple of kids. Agreeing that future rendezvous will take place at my house.

After these back-seat adventures, Josey and I text daily. "*Good morning.*" "*How are you?*" We joke, we banter, sometimes talk on the phone. I enjoy the connection.

Maybe, this is how a bond forms, but I still feel something missing.

***

~16~

There is a barrage of online threats by a few disgruntled members of George's former motorcycle club. Mainly because we are opening the show at the Rubicon theater in Ventura, his old stomping grounds and just up the road from the Ventura chapter of the Angels and their clubhouse. His manager proposes security but George scoffs at the idea. Besides, security is expensive, and we are on a low budget. Images of brawls, firebombs and mass shootings fill the writer's imagination while George straddles the stage defiantly, in customary black shorts and high black socks and Nike trainers, preparing for his theatrical debut.

The Rubicon, a two-hundred seat theater that was once a church, is sold out; it's a full house.

Finally, first night arrives, and Josey arrives with it, bearing roses in white, yellow and red in appreciation of writer and star. She's a supporter and I appreciate it. There's a lot to like about Josey, and friends with benefits is looking more like a relationship, or the beginning of one.

Many of my other friends also attend, including the Tribal Elder and his wife, along with my property lawyer. No cardiologist, which is just as well since my blood pressure is soaring and my heart is beating like a kick drum in four-three-five time. Plus, I have an appointment with him in a week.

Nervous, because I'm overseeing the sound cues from a small room above the stage; in fact, I seem more on edge than George, who has traded his black shorts for black jeans and is seated calmly in his dressing room, with Josey's roses in a vase on his dressing table, waiting for the curtain to rise.

I wish him luck, then walk through the audience, who are now finding their seats, then up the stairs leading to the sound booth.

Sitting beside the two sound technicians, looking down at the crowd through the big, squared window of my perch. Spotting Josey and a couple of her friends seated within two rows of the Elder. I have purposely not introduced them for fear of a penciled notation on his legal pad.

The music begins, an instrumental number from the *Pat Garrett and Billy The Kid* album; it's the real Bob Dylan, and the show's on.

A powerful overhead beam hits stage left, leaving a circular zone of pure white light against the matt black floor.

Problem is, George should be standing in the center of that pure light, but he's not.

A hush falls over the Rubicon as the show begins, or at least it should begin, if only George was on stage.

Cue the voice soundtrack, supposed to be the voice of a judge, asking if George has something to say before being sentenced by the court. In fact, it's my voice, recorded and echoing through the sound system.

Where is George?

The voice of the Judge continues.

I'm worried. Has he been assassinated in his dressing room by an enraged ex-brother bearing a bouquet of lilies? Garroted before he can draw his knives?

George, where are you?

The answer is he's backstage, in the dark, behind the curtain, trying like hell to find an opening in the heavy burlap. But we don't know this.

We just know we're in trouble.

The techs look over at me. I grimace and shrug my shoulders. See the producer staring up towards the window-box. Sheer panic on his face.

George?

Please?

My voice, the Judge's voice, has nearly reached the part where I ask for his words to the court.

Ten seconds away.

Five.

George?

This is a disaster.

And then, a miracle … The man in black appears. From the opposite side of the stage. Shuffling slowly into view.

Arriving beneath the spotlight just in time, greeted by a burst of applause from his friends and family who are seated in the front rows. The rest of the theater joins in. It's a standing ovation, even the Elder and his wife are on their feet, and George has yet to say a word.

And, when he does, he's flawless, convincing, concluding with: "Over time I have tried to become smarter, wiser and more tempered. I've not always taken the correct turns in life but when I have realized I was off course I have always tried my best to once again find true north."

Another standing ovation.

He's Hamlet in black.

A star is born.

*

Euphoria reigns at the end of the performance. I feel we've truly achieved something. Proud of George. Proud of myself. The Rubicon is already sold out for the next show as Josey and I head back to my place for our own celebration, which includes a long mirror, hauled painstakingly from my gym and up the winding staircase and placed beside my bed. Resulting in the personal revelation that my ass is as flat as a pancake. I can't see hers because of our Kama Sutra positioning, but before I can change it for a better view, her cell phone rings.

It's mama, in the midst of a panic attack.

Josey leaves abruptly, and I am left to lug the mirror back to the gym and finish my celebrations alone.

Am I falling in love?

I'd like to say yes, even try to convince myself that I am, but I don't think so. There's a connection that I just don't feel, even though I try to talk myself into it. She's attractive. She's smart. Her ass is less flat than mine. She's attentive, an accomplished bedroom athlete, but because of her work schedule and her mother, not very available. Always with that cell phone. Poised for an emergency. Always that feeling that she is just about to leave. And she's bossy. Forever the chef, always in control. Even the bedside mirror was her idea. I didn't really want to watch my flat ass bobbing up and down.

Am I listening?

Am I learning?

Is this what love after fifty, sixty or seventy feels like, an arrangement, a friend with benefits? Am I being immature, waiting for that high-school high, when just being around the supposed magical other makes everything possible and life just about perfect?

I don't know.

Maybe this is it. As good as it gets.

And even this gets better. Josey and I spend a domestic evening watching movies on Netflix at my house; go to the Santa Barbara zoo, drink whiskey sours in a bar in Palm Springs, spend a night in a Palm Desert hotel and bathe in the hot springs. Send each other "good morning" greetings and emojis of hearts and kisses.

But something is missing, and when that something is a soul connection it's tough to fake. I don't know if she feels this, and I don't ask, because I'm not sure what I want, and if whatever that may be is actually out there.

*

Following the glories of opening night, and my lusty performance in the gym mirror, I endure a fear-packed visit to the cardiologist, and another echo scan. In and out after the scan, driving away as if I'm escaping a medieval torture chamber. Appointment scheduled in three days to discuss the results.

"You have a good strong heart," the doctor says.

It may not beat in normal time, the valve may leak, but the damn thing's still kicking.

"Surgery?"

He looks at me and smiles.

He prescribes a blood thinner and says, "See you in a year."

I drive out of the carpark as if I've just been issued a reprieve from execution.

One year. Anything can happen in a year. I may even fall in love.

*

George is in St. Louis, Missouri, playing to half-full houses and looking for new management.

I'm stuck in the middle, trying to get paid while pieces of the original stage set litter my driveway. I threaten to throw them out. His manager says, go ahead, but the posters and large wooden frames are too heavy to haul to the street. I'd rather lift a full-length mirror to my bedroom.

The prospects of *Outlaw* making it to New York seem unlikely; and I'm glad we didn't order those hundred thousand T-shirts. Still, I had a great time, and heard things that no other man alive has ever heard. Including phone calls from George saying he loves doing the show and would like to just keep on going, riding that road to forever, if only the houses were full.

Josey and I continue to see each other when we can, but mama and work make it an unpredictable coupling; still, after a three-week hiatus we schedule dinner at a Santa Barbara restaurant, after which we plan a night together at a seaside hotel in Carpentaria. It's the same one I occupied with Michelle, way back in the days of crotchless striped jumpsuits when I thought that this dating game would be easy, and the world was my oyster. I'm hoping we don't get the same room, for sentimental reasons, and also hope that no one recognizes me as the drunken geezer with the loud guitar.

The rich tomato-saffron garlic stew with cod is fine, despite Josey's complaints that the fish is overdone; and I've cut back, courtesy of the ER doctor, to one glass of red while Josey has two glasses of white; but she's not driving, and I seem permanently traumatized by the Asian cop, so one glass is my limit. Still, I'm feeling good and Josey looks pretty in the candlelight; it's been a long time and her bedroom acrobatics shadow dance in my mind, an exquisite erotica, in shades of gray. Yes, I'm really looking forward to that seaside hotel, the salt air, the sound of the surf, an intimate room, a warm bed, ready to call the server and pay the bill, when I notice a shift in Josey's face; it's an expression, somewhere between surprise and downright shock. I've never seen it before. Her skin changes color, from a healthy pinkish glow to the snow-white shades of the rafter. I turn to see the object of her attention; a stooped, gray-haired woman, standing in the doorway, looks like she's wearing a nightgown, wild-eyed. Staring at us.

Josey's voice sounds choked, words squeezed from the back of her throat, "Oh God, it's my mother."

"How did she get here?" I ask.

Josey is already on her feet. Moving fast.

"I told her where I'd be. Now I've got to get her home."

I watch as they depart, caring daughter's arm wrapped round a shuffling old lady, soothing her with words. The door closes slowly, and they are gone.

I'm left alone. Sobered. Sorry for Josey and aware of the obligation she has taken on. Thinking of the vacant room at the seaside hotel and feeling just about the same way, empty. Questioning. Will it always be this way? I cannot condemn her for caring for her mother, or working long hours, or bossing me around the bedroom, well, maybe for that, but I've got to care for me. What do I need? Maybe it's not a friend with benefits, or not this particular friend, someone I see every now and again, with no real platform to build a relationship upon, someone I am fond of but sense no deep connection to. So, where does this leave us? Where does it leave me?

Am I listening?

Am I being honest?

Am I learning anything?

*

Outlaw plays two more shows, a homage to our small town and local theater. By now, George and his manger are outright feuding, and just before the final performance, the manager storms off, taking the sound cues, which are on his computer, with him, never to return, back to wherever he came from, somewhere East of Eden, a long way from the bright lights of Broadway. We borrow a computer, hire a local computer whiz, and concoct our own sound system; the show must go on.

The theater is packed; George delivers a tour de force, suddenly veering off into unscripted improvisations. Telling stories that I've never heard. Stories that no one has ever heard, and perhaps will never hear again. Stories that he may have never heard. Two hours in and he's still rolling. Pacing the stage; punching into the air, gesturing with his hands. Fighting wars and dodging bullets. I'm waiting for the knives to appear when George magically returns to the script, delivering the final lines of his soliloquy.

"I have always been an outlaw ...

Yes, that judge was right. Only God does know what I've gotten away with.

And only God knows what I've paid ..."

And, with those prophetic words ... the lights fade to black and *Outlaw* is history.

Josey is on her feet, for the third time in as many shows, loyal and supportive. Joining in for the encore as the outlaw returns for a bow, well, actually an extended series of bows. Shaking hands with the fans, before vanishing into the night.

Little did I know, but that was the last time I would see George, other than passing him in the street with a quick hello, before he left to shoot a TV series in Spain, no doubt telling someone, somewhere, things that he has never told another living creature.

*

Josey and I drive back to my house and after a celebratory glass of champagne, Josey lays it on the line. Her face is serious, and I guess I should have seen it coming. The emoji kisses, the flowers, the good morning greetings, the hands in prayer, the happy faces with hearts for eyes. Yes, I should have seen it. One of us has been taking this thing between us very seriously, and that one is not me. Josey has been loyal, supportive and a friend, but my friend with benefits is about to change the game. Maybe she already has, but I didn't notice.

Seated upon the same sofa that only seven months ago launched our athletic forays into the upper regions of my home, including dancing naked to country songs, stripteases, raucous laughter, and a mutual agreement that this was just for sex, just for fun, just for the time-being, playtime is over. Josey's in the kitchen, and I'm about to become the saffron risotto.

She declares that we are, indeed, having a relationship; we go to dinner, we go to hotels, watch movies, listen to music, have sex, enjoy conversation. I agree; it's a relationship, all right. So why do I question it? Why does it not feel natural? It's not her mother, although she plays a part. It's not her cat, who is wheezing but still chasing squirrels. So, what is it, what is missing?

I'm asking myself this when she answers for me. Explaining that certain things have been lacking from my etiquette, and she wants them put right. Rule one: Always ask how her day has gone before talking about my own. Understood. Rule two: Never interrupt her when she is speaking, which I am prone to do. Understood. Rule three: Never glance down at my pinging cell phone to check a message when in her presence; something that she is allowed to do because of her mother, but when I do it; it's a sign of disrespect. Agreed ... And finally, Josey tells me that she will be unavailable for the next three months because of commitments at work, her mother's growing needs, and the ailing cat who may expire at any moment or live another several years.

Understood.

We part at my front door, with a quick kiss; there's a moment of hesitation.

"Josey," I say. "This isn't going to work."

She looks at me, incredulous. "What isn't going to work?"

"This. You and me, or you, me, your mother and your cat."

Her face changes; arching eyebrows, clenched jaw. Her voice is trembling. "Are you dumping me?"

Beyond her spectacular shoulders, the Hummer awaits. I'm wondering if she'll throw it into gear and ram my front door.

"I am saying that our relationship does not work."

"Same thing," she hisses.

"Yes, then that's what I'm saying."

Her anger is palpable, and, for a moment, I expect her to smack me. Instead, she says, "Fine." Turns and marches towards the Hummer. "I never want to see you again, ever!" she shouts as she slams the door. Tossing gravel as she drives away, into the long, loveless night.

***

~17~

Alone again, by choice.

But why do I keep making this choice?

Sitting here, at my kitchen table, dining on a can of Amy's organic lentil soup, discovered on the shelf of my local health food store, with pita chips on the side. Watching as night falls and the rain pelts my windows, tempted to text Josey to ask if she'd like a sleepover; now that I've mastered sexual intercourse in the downward dog position, I'm hopeful we can move into a full lotus. I'm sure she'd hang up on me.

Sex?

As Josey once said, "I can find that in the parking lot of Trader Joe's." Well, I'm not certain if I can match her on that, although I must look provocative in my baggy sweats, pushing my orange shopping cart down the aisle, alongside the bananas; but I get the point. It isn't sex, it's the connection.

Companionship? Yes, that would be great too, but after all these years and all these patterns, how do I find a set of patterns that match my own? Maybe it's wounds binding with other wounds in an attempt to mutually heal. Where are you, partner? I'm right over here, shouting "fat ass" and bleeding.

And Love? That's the big one.

That takes risking it all. Not playing the numbers. Off the sites. Out of the game. Walking the tightrope without a safety net.

But love often comes with her sidekick, pain, because love is vulnerability. Love is honest.

Yes. I know all the words, all the platitudes. I've read them; memorized them. Recited them a thousand times, written them, but living them, that's another story.

Eat my lentils. Restrain from visiting the dating sites. No messages. No profiles. No studying faces, before blowing them up by spreading my fingers against the screen or pondering legs and asses and breasts. The possibility of finding someone special is always out there and the temptation is great. Forget about Angelina and her well-developed pelvic floor. Forget about Kristan and her built-in champagne cork. Forget about Josey and her long, wide shoes. God, I hated those shoes.

I've got a can full of Amy and my garlic pita bread. Sip it. Eat it. Go to bed. Sleep restlessly. Get up. Meditate. Quiet the monkey mind.

Request an audience with the Elder. Granted. Three o'clock. I'm there on the dot. He has a doorway chinning bar in his office. I take a grip and perform a quick eighteen, up and down, like my moods. Look at the Elder, who's is looking at me; his eyes suggesting medication, perhaps a mild sedative. Dream interpretation? A warning about catastrophizing. Cautioning that everything is not all just black and white. Stop living in extremes. Have we tried hypnosis?

I'm breathing hard after the pull-ups, adrenalized. Fight or flight, I'll take fight. Another extreme, bring it on. The legal pad. The list. The indelible ink.

"Please, sit down," the Elder suggests. Then, before I can ask. "No, I am not going to take your blood pressure. If you could do what you just did, you're fine."

"That's debatable," I say, feeling like I could expire at any moment, settling into the soft sofa, my home away from home, my mountaintop retreat in red velvet.

During the course of my hour, and as I knew it would, the list appears, and for a change, I don't wince. Watching calmly as Josey's name is recorded. "Yes, that's an *ey*, not an *ie*. Wondering when my own name will finally be added, to commemorate my promised rebirth, from Dick to Richard.

"Take some time off," he says. "Go back, have another look at yourself; spend more time alone."

Sentenced, by the Elder, to solitary confinement ... again. How could he do this to me, after several years in his presence and eighteen chins on his doorway bar?

"And when you feel fear, or panic, or intense sadness, sit with it," he adds. "Allow it to pass through you, because it will, and by sitting with it and not denying it or running away, you are exercising your emotional muscles."

I have been doing this, this emotional acceptance thing, during my morning meditations, and he's correct, emotions do rise and fall, and they do pass through. But I have never thought of this practice as a form of exercise, and never considered the emotions as muscles; yet when I do, the idea makes sense: if I can exercise my biceps and back on a doorway chinning bar, I can exercise my emotional muscles by working with the weight of sorrow, despair, longing and fear.

*

Life in my kitchen continues with intimate dinner parties, attended by myself, and Amy, who comes in a wide variety from lentil to cream of mushroom and opens conveniently from the top. Throw in a bag of Jan's organic yellow sweet potato chips and life in solitary is becoming an art form, as day by day, night by night I develop my emotional muscles. Though, if I had to use these new muscles to pull my body up on the chinning bar, I figure I'd get about three repetitions before failure. I sense improvement. Prior to training, I'd simply hang, weighted down by my ego in all its bruised splendor. These last years have altered that, created a few modifications, and if the ego is a suit of clothes to be worn in public, I've just removed my fancy pants. Replacing them with a loincloth. Going primitive.

Am I listening?

Am I learning?

Yes, I've learned that my external system is definitely stronger than my internal system. At this point, I am more image than essence, more skin than snake, but that is changing. I feel a metamorphosis as the snake gradually makes his appearance, all raw and pink and sensitive.

*

Finally, I resume checking the sites, but the desperation has gone. I'm an old hand at this game and can browse without buying. More interested in what the woman has to say, in her written profile, than in the quality of the often photoshopped pictures. Yes, there needs to be an initial attraction, but that is the image; what she writes about herself is the essence. I read these profiles, and then I read them again, realizing that I am far from alone in this business of being single.

One more stop on my road to self-discovery, and that's to my friend Elaine, a quintessential California girl, pretty and blonde and vivacious, and just about as eccentric as I am. She's nearly as old, too, and we've spent many hours in her metaphysical emporium, amidst candles and Buddhas and embroidered tapestries, discussing life, and our lives in particular.

I first met Elaine when I was renovating my house, needed some objects of art, and was drawn to the displays in her windows, long candlesticks, wicker tables, hand-painted birds on fabric swatches, her own paintings of cityscapes, country fields and flowers, childlike in their simplicity and bright honest colors, yet so skilled in their execution, hanging above pieces of sculpture. Just my taste, simple and eclectic but sophisticated at the same time. One piece in particular caught my eye, a cast figure of Cupid, god of attraction and affection; he looked like he was made from bronze. I felt I needed him. In fact, I knew I needed him. Had to have him.

Opened the door and entered a pine scented warp in time, orchestrated by '60s folk artist Donovan singing, *Must be the season of the witch.*

Elaine entered from a door leading to her living area in the back of the shop. All smiles, paisley print and grooving like a '60s go-go girl, hips swaying, arms moving like twin cobras, as Donovan sang, *Beatniks out to make it rich.*

Giggling. "Did you come for a reading?"

"Reading?"

"A Tarot reading?"

"No, I came for the Cupid."

Lifting him from the shelf. Lighter than I'd imagined, and more fragile, made of plaster, not bronze. Handing him to Elaine so she could take him behind the register and give me a price. And, somewhere, between my grip and hers, the son of love dropped to the floor. Head snapping off, clean as a decapitation by a French guillotine.

Silence.

I looked down. Cupid's face looked up at me. Pleading. Don't leave me here. I'm wounded, but I'm yours.

"I'm sorry," I said. "That was my fault. I still want him. He can be repaired. How much is he?"

Elaine laughed, while Joni Mitchell began "Big Yellow Taxi" from somewhere behind the floral sundresses and rainbow scarves on a nearby rack.

"I'm not going to charge you for him," she said. "If you want him, he's a gift."

If she only knew how appropriate that gift was, but neither of us did at the time. I had never really been on my own, never been on the online circuit, looking for a real connection, and had no idea what to expect.

Cupid was a natural fit with Superglue, and within hours the formerly decapitated son of love was reunited with his head, standing in one piece on top of my Chinese chest, next to a stone carved Buddha from Thailand. The Buddha and the Cupid, strange bedfellows, wisdom and love, soulmates in their own special way.

*

The Tarot reading did not take place for another three years, and only after I'd filled my house with silk flowers, porcelain pots, embroidered tapestries, that wicker table, two long candlesticks, a painted bird on cloth and a small earthen colored clay monkey who sits in a meditative posture beside my fireplace, staring up at the Chinese chest and waiting for Cupid to deliver on his promise.

And ... All of the above at a ten percent family discount.

*

The reading.

Elaine and I sit in wooden chairs at a small, squared table in her curtained parlor, an anteroom that divides her shop from her living space.

She hands me the brightly colored deck.

I shuffle.

Lay the cards on the table, face down. Pick one, hand it to Elaine. She turns it over. Another, until we have a five-card spread.

She smiles. Saying, "There you are," as she points to a crowned king in red robes, seated on a golden throne. "This is so good ... the King of Wands. That's a beautiful card, and it's Sagittarius, your sign. He's full of energy, and he gets what he's after. That's you."

Me?

The King?

Going to get what I'm after?

I feel a surge. An alpha male unleashed. Empowered. Reassured.

What is it I'm after? To get the hell off the dating sites. I'm tired, bored and despite attempts at correction, my age is still eight years younger than I actually am. An online fraudster, in pursuit of younger women, most on Social Security. Robbing the cradle.

Pick another card and hand it over.

Elaine lays it down beside the King of Wands.

Her smile broadens.

"And there she is."

Excitement builds.

"Who?"

"The Queen of Wands. Your equal. You were made for each other. A great partner. She's been waiting for you."

Somewhere, from another dimension, Cupid winks and whispers, "Thanks for the superglue."

Elaine continues, "She's a strong, compassionate woman, very kind, nurturing, and a fire sign, like you ... Oh, this is wonderful. Be patient, she's on her way. Just a little more time to go." Flipping another card.

My heart fills with hope. Going through every woman I know, like a checklist before lift-off. Champagne corks. Blue woks. Hummers. Silicone breasts. Red thongs. Massive tongues. Fat asses. Black Teslas ... Sorry, my eyes are going, that's actually a

Chevy Volt. But I can't remember what any of their signs are, and doubt if I even asked. Still, I don't believe there's a Queen amongst them. Oh yes, there was one, with an Adam's apple and size twelve shoes. But somebody new? That's even more exciting.

Elaine studies the card.

"There's some distance between you, and some time, but she's coming. Be patient."

Patience? Not a virtue. I'm practicing, but I'm struggling. I want it now. End this dance, once and for all. The Queen of Wands is on her way. I'll go home and clean the house. Polish things up. Light a fire. Open a bottle of wine. Get ready.

Thanks Elaine. Hug her. Tell her I love her. Drive into the starry night, riding a silver cloud of hope. Winging up the long driveway, past the old oak tree. Inside. A nod to Cupid. You did it. She's coming. Thanks.

The euphoria leads to seven hours of sleep. No dreams of ex-wives, passionate kisses or riding bicycles into trees. No dreams at all, or none that I remember.

First thing in the morning, I type in my password, and I'm online.

***

~18~

I became a psychology major in college, when, in the late '60s, it was infinitely more hip to smoke weed and drop LSD with your psych professor than to sit in a class on modern literature and discuss the "phallic power" and hidden symbols inside D.H. Lawrence's *Lady Chatterley's Lover.*

I loved gamekeeper Oliver Mellors and tales of his ever-ready penis, also known as John Thomas, and the way he illicitly pleasured the married Lady Constance Chatterley, but nowhere near as much as I loved getting stoned with Professor Rogers and listening to a stereo mix of Jimi Hendrix's *Electric Ladyland,* followed by a discussion on mind expansion, telepathy, and the evidence of self-fulfilling prophecy. In other words, if someone connects with your mind, and plants an idea, you are likely to attempt to fulfill that idea, or make it come true.

Which leads to my renewed obsession with online dating, and hopefully the manifestation of the Queen of Wands.

Evidence of my desperation?

I don't think so, because I don't feel desperate. Vigilant is a better word, plus it's a little bit of fun, trying to link a face with a card. Feeling it out.

My first Queen is from Laurel Canyon in Los Angeles; and, ultimately, costs me dearly, in the form of my treasured, black Calvin Klein boxer shorts with the buttoned fly front. Luckily, I bought a three-pack.

*

It all begins with good intent. Rachel has viewed me and pressed the "like" button. I check out her profile, her photographic résumé, wonderful smile, her age, given as sixty but later found to be seventy. Doesn't matter; I'm going for substance and sustainability, not kids in their sixties. Maturity is what I'm after. Occupation: massage therapist, specializing in Rolfing. I've had that once and it hurt, so I'll stay off her table, at least till I get to know her.

I send a message, inquiring as to her birth sign. She answers, Leo. That's a fire sign. I'm on. Heating up. Then dispense with the traditional exchange of numbers and hour-long phone calls and request an immediate lunch. No beating round the bush. Armed with the secret Tarot reading and backed by a plaster cupid with a three-hundred-and-sixty-degree acrylic scar around his neck, I feel ready to charge in and meet my queen.

Lunch is agreed, a restaurant chosen, the Infiniti cleaned and vacuumed, clothing selected.

I'm off.

To Malibu and a round table with a red and white squared cloth, sea breeze and ocean views. Sipping a glass of rosé when Rachel arrives. She's petite and blonde, with that warm online smile and an interesting collage of age spots on her left hand that seems to coincide with a similar pattern on my right. Could this be a sign? Something from the Zodiac, maybe an undiscovered constellation?

Another rosé and I'm beginning to believe it is. We continue to chat. Recounting tales of online dates and the surprises that often await at the end of a long drive to a restaurant or coffee shop at some mutually agreed midway point. And, being California, a distance of thirty or forty miles is about an average midway point. So is a charge of a hundred and twenty dollars on a credit card, so I'm really hoping that the Queen appears before the King is too broke to continue his pursuit. Conversation continues. She's very open and feels honest and vulnerable. Aside from being one of the original Rolfers, and a direct student of the originator Ida Rolf, Rachel is also a published author, a musician, and, like me, a child of the sixties.

"I'm glad we met," she says at the end of a relaxed lunch. "Maybe it's fate."

Fate? Wait till Elaine hears this.

I walk her to her car, a vintage Toyota Land Cruiser, and she kisses me. No champagne cork here, this is soft and yielding, a 1948 Chateau Lafite Rothschild, all red berries and earthy notes, aged in a seasoned oak barrel.

"I'll phone you," she promises.

And, two days later, she does.

I'm excited to hear her voice, but more excited when she invites me to spend the night at her place in Laurel Canyon; I assume it's not separate beds but don't ask. This is a woman who doesn't mess around; I guess at this age there's no point. Consider a quick consultation with Elaine, who is now working in conjunction with the Elder, although he doesn't know it, but decide to wait till after the weekend in order to gather data, give a full report and possibly get a re-shuffle.

"And bring your guitar," she suggests.

A musical evening. Who could ask for more?

Three o'clock finally comes. I shave and shower and dress. Here come those Calvin Kleins. I always save the classic button fly fronts for important occasions, of which there have been few lately, so my newest, blackest pair are folded and waiting in my closet. On they go, followed by my jeans and an old faded blue silk shirt, a relic from the sixties; it feels appropriate.

Grab my overnight bag, grab my guitar. Into the car, plug the address into the nav and pull out of town. Feeling like a twenty-one-year-old, on my way to a date with Raquel Welch.

*

Rachel's house is on the left side of a mountainous road that branches off the main drag leading to Mulholland Drive; the road is narrow, barely room for two cars to pass, and has houses on either side, some modernized and immaculate, others that look like they haven't been touched since Jim Morrison, Frank Zappa and a host of '60s rockers inhabited the area. The place definitely has soul. There's reefer on the wind, and my guitar is playing itself from the backseat. I pull into her short driveway. Open the door. Get out. Roll my hips in an attempt to straighten my back, bend forward and try to touch my toes, making it half-way, roll my knees in an effort to walk. Hoping she's not watching from a window. Realizing that there's nothing less appealing than having to assist your new lover to his feet after a two-hour car ride, then having to support his stooped body as he enters your home, guitar quivering in his liver-spotted right hand.

Not to worry; because Rachel's not home. The house, in need of repair, is empty. Maybe she's out Rolfing someone in the canyon, but why didn't she let me know? I check the address. Seems I'm in the right place. Right on time, but what now? Peer in the old leaded glass windows. See thick Persian carpets. Mandalas hanging on the walls. A piano. A cello. What looks like a set of tribal drums, a worn sofa, a sitar, some meditation cushions, all suitable for the King and the Queen of a certain era, perhaps King Crimson. There's nothing left to do but wait. Be cool. Pull my guitar from the car, sit down on a rickety metal chair on her front porch and play like I'm auditioning for Crosby, Stills and Nash, all former residents of the canyon.

Fifteen minutes into my solo concert, featuring a heartfelt rendition of Dylan's "Heaven's Door," and the dark green Land Cruiser pulls in behind the black Infiniti; Rachel disembarks, lugging a massage table. I'm up to assist. Grateful to have done those preliminary stretching exercises, but still careful not to pull anything vital. After all, the evening is yet to come.

Inside, the house is bigger than I thought, not too wide but deep, with rooms in the back and a spiral staircase leading upstairs. A quick salad, a glass or two of wine and the music begins. I receive a serenade on Rachel's cello, deep and moody, then perform on my guitar. Luckily, I'm well-rehearsed from the wait on her porch and the fingers flow. She says she likes my feel for the instrument and suggests we dance. No problem, I've rolled and loosened my knees so they should be stable enough for a slow number.

Eric Clapton sings "You look wonderful tonight" as we embrace and move like two old groovers in four-four time. About to close my eyes, thinking of a gentle kiss, when a deep male voice shatters the moment.

"Hey, bro?"

I turn.

He's tall, black, and wears a tight red T-shirt with the single word, "STRANGE" written in white letters across the front.

Looming above me with a shaved head and a very wide smile. Friendly enough, but how did he get in, and what does he want?

He extends his fist, obviously requesting a bump. I oblige, noting that his hand could probably swallow two of mine.

"Nelson," he says. "What's yours?"

Meanwhile, the music continues, and Rachel doesn't seem to notice the intrusion. Dancing on her own, eyes closed, while I deal with the mystery man.

"My name's Richard."

Another bump.

"Cool ... Enjoy."

And, with that, Nelson pivots and disappears, up the single step leading to the entranceway. Sharp right; headed to the spiral staircase.

Not wanting to douse the magic, I return to dancing, but it doesn't take long before my timing is interrupted by another stranger, at least to me, who enters through the front door. He's an older gentleman, reminding me of the actor Christopher Lloyd in *Back to the Future*, with long, wispy silver hair, dressed in a gray striped suit and as delicate in stature as Nelson is strong, attached to two miniature white poodles by a long leash; he doesn't so much as glance in our direction as he whispers by and continues up the stairs. Passed by a college-aged girl with a basket of laundry on her way down.

"I rent rooms," Rachel explains as the music ends.

Okay, I get it. Nothing wrong with making a little additional income to augment the Rolfing. Just a surprise.

The evening continues as we sit in front of a log fire in an adjoining room. A kiss or two, a tickling of tongues, but romance is difficult when Nelson keeps popping in and out, on his way to and from the kitchen, requesting fist bumps and brotherly salutations. I think he's either very stoned or increasingly inebriated as his "hey bro's" have transitioned into a sequence of "dudes," but a lengthier version, like "doooood" to accompany an increasingly vigorous bump.

Finally, Rachel suggests we adjourn to her bedroom.

I follow her up the spiral staircase, and nod hello to the wispy-haired older gentleman from Back to the Future on his way down, minus the poodles. Sharp right at the top and down a long corridor leading to a room that appears to have been hit by a bomb. Clothes scattered, papers and books in heaps and what appears to be an assortment of medical equipment lying on the floor, including a stethoscope and a blood pressure cuff, perhaps to check my vitals before anything strenuous occurs.

Elaine, I really need to talk to you about that Tarot reading. Perhaps an over the phone consultation. Either that or an emergency call to the Tribal Elder, requesting an immediate evacuation plan.

Push these thoughts out of my mind.

Inhale. Exhale, pause.

Clam down.

Sit on the edge of the bed, remove my shoes while Rachel disappears into the adjoining bathroom, reappearing in a pale blue night dress. Very feminine. She turns off the overhead light, lights a candle and slides in beneath the disheveled top sheet, bolstering herself against a pillow, as she looks at me in the flickering light. Shoes and socks off, midway through pulling down my jeans when I hear the sound of footsteps in the hallway.

The footsteps recede, fading down the staircase as I continue, jeans gone, '60s silk shirt discarded, and finally the black, button fronted Kleins. Off they come, tossed like a stripper's bra into the already sizeable pile of clothing on the floor.

Let the passion begin.

Or not.

Generally, I don't lack rhythm. I love music. I love dancing. I love being physical, but I cannot get this one together. Our kisses don't gel, certainly not like the day of the Chateau Lafite, or even down on the sofa; in the bedroom, it's Hard Kombucha as our bodies move in an idiosyncratic counter-time, plainly not in unison. She goes left; I go left and a half; she goes up; I go up too, but higher, then come crashing down.

I hear a drum, deep and resonating. Must be someone playing that thing in the living room, resembling a tall wooden mushroom. Bending what's left of my mind. Transporting me to a '50s porno flick in black and white, where the guys all wore over the calf black nylon socks and garters. With Nelson, master or percussion, on the skins.

"My God, we are sexually incompatible," I tell myself, digging deep into my coital archives for some love-saving maneuver and coming up dry. Realizing that this could all be my fault. Overthinking. Victim of the monkey mind. Struggling mentally to find some form of a physical common ground. No luck.

And, all the while, Rachel dances the jitterbug beneath me while I attempt an impassioned tango from the top, as below decks, the beat goes on.

Until at last, I give up and roll over. Feeling like a flop.

Rachel doesn't say a word. Simply blows out the candle and pulls up the comforter and snuggles into her pillow; her gentle snores remind me of a cat purring.

The drumming stalls then grinds to a halt; I envision Nelson, passed out and draped over the big wooden mushroom.

Morning comes. I've had very little rest and feel like a quick exit is essential. I'm sort of embarrassed. Like I've let the team down. Can we have a do-over?

Rachel seems fine. Pops out of bed, straightens her back with a bending, twisting move that I'm familiar with and use frequently, slips on a pink, terrycloth bathrobe and says, "See you downstairs."

I grab my jeans, pull them on quickly, put on my socks and shoes, separate the vintage faded blue silk shirt from the vintage pile of laundry on the floor, step over the blood pressure cuff and head down.

Coffee, toast and marmalade on the breakfast table. Classical music crackling from an old-fashioned tubed radio that resides on the shelf.

Eat, drink, quick kiss, thank you Rachel.

Up the 101 freeway, headed north, sixty miles from the canyon and sixty miles from home when I realize that something's missing. And it's not my guitar. No, it's the Calvin Kleins, which in my haste I forgot about, and they will now join the growing pile of undergarments on the floor of Rachel's bedroom. Is this how she accumulates that multi-colored cotton mound? How many Kleins have been before me? Who will inherit the buttoned fly? Nelson, please, they're yours, my gift in return for the drumming.

But will I see Rachel again?

Probably not.

Is Rachel the Queen of Wands? Yes, for someone, but not this crusty old King, riding the desert highways, sans underwear, balls bouncing against the saddle, traveling to whatever comes next.

A pitstop at Elaine's, just to report in, and to issue an in-person complaint about the misguided Tarot. She listens to my tales of Rachel, and finally a confession of my inability to make love in a royal fashion. Appearing mortified, but in an amused way.

"Well, I can't believe I was that far off, let's take another look," she says, guiding me to the reading room. Once inside and seated in the straight-backed chairs, she says, "Shuffle, then pick another card." I do, and low and behold, the Queen of Wands stares up at us from the purple tablecloth. I'm thinking that Elaine may be playing with a loaded deck. Even she appears surprised. "She's still out there," she says, as Cupid smiles from afar.

I leave on a magic carpet, the words "still out there," playing like a shamanic flute in my mind.

The Elder is more pragmatic.

"Why do you keep doing this to yourself?" he asks, after I describe my latest adventure.

I hum, haw and refrain from mentioning the Queen of Wands, or my latest visit to Elaine's. Considering this omission as a professional courtesy. The last thing I need at a time like this is conflicting points of view, since I have several of my own, and all of mine are conflicting.

Then … The list appears, as if it has become an extension of his left hand, the Bic growing like a thin blue finger from his right. I watch as he writes "Rachel" on the hallowed paper, right beneath Josey, although in what appears to be smaller letters, perhaps to signify the comparative brevity of this last fling.

~19~

Queen number 2.

Rebel shows her face, online, less than a week later. I'm moving faster now, straight from a "like" on the site to a scheduled phone call, and, if the call goes well, out to a candlelit dinner. No messing around for the King of Wands.

This potential Queen is dark-haired, very good looking in a sassy rock 'n roll kind of way, well-dressed, bosomy, and has, perhaps, had a bit of tasteful cosmetic surgery in the region of her nose, which is just a little too perfect, and her eyes, which look a little too wrinkle free, but as I know all too well, these photos may be a decade old, or even older. In fact, it may not even be her.

I'm becoming a cynic.

Our phone conversation reveals a slight southern drawl, making it no surprise when she tells me she's originally from Atlanta, Georgia. I am surprised, however, when she asks if I am still capable of sexual activity. I guess that's fair enough considering my age, but I do note that older women seem less inhibited about asking very personal questions, and are very forthright as to what they require in the bedroom; tempting me to supply Josey as a reference, with performance data included, but unsure if the bitterly departed chef would do me any favors.

Conversation moves fluidly from the bedroom to the boardroom; Rebel is an insurance broker and owns her own agency. I mention a few of the books I have written, none that she's ever heard of, while neglecting to say that my last was published over eight years ago. Lately, I seem to have run out of ideas; either that, or all my creative energy has been diverted to the online hunt for a needle in a haystack.

"I could retire now and have enough money to live on for ten years without doing a thing," she adds. I do a quick calculation, figuring that beats me by about nine, then consider asking her to take me to dinner; but no, that's not my style. I am, after all, the King of Wands. Drinks on me. Dinners on me. Wine. Caviar. Want a cigar?

Tired of the search. The phone calls. The driving. The coffee. The dinners. The credit cards. The anticipation. The let-downs. I'm tired of all the baggage. Mothers, cats, dogs, kids, temperamental guinea pigs, bi-polar disorders, alcohol, dementia, ex-husbands. Then there's my own baggage. Obsessive behavior. Fantasizing. Catastrophizing. Fear. Panic. Will I ever see her again? Will she ever call? What did I do to turn her off? Too needy? Too possessive? Too intense? What did I just say?

I'm really tired of it, and so must be my close friends who put up with me bleating down the phone about my latest let-downs, spiritual revelations and heartaches. Yet, I keep going, like a marathoner at the twenty-mile mark, hitting the wall; give me a sip of water, the scent of perfume, the hint of a nipple through a silk blouse, the outline of a thong through tight yoga pants, the words, "I love you," and, low and behold, I've got my second wind.

I know she's out there, that magical other, that Queen Of Wands.

Rebel, here I come.

*

The restaurant is in Westlake Village, a stone's throw for me, which means forty-nine miles, but who's counting anymore? I arrive at six-thirty; we're scheduled to meet at seven and this gives me time to pick a quiet table at the back of the outdoor patio, suitable for eye-gazing and private conversation, have a glass of Pinot, suitable for consciousness-numbing, and prepare for Rebel, wondering how she will compare to her photos and, at this point, not really caring. I am basically going through the motions. Discouraged. Jaded. Telling myself that this is the last one, my swan song. When it's over I'll go home. Grow a beard. Open several bottles of red wine simultaneously. Sit down at my computer and become a writer, again. Because this just isn't worth it.

Ping?

A text. "In the car park. Be there in five."

Even now, as drained as they must be, my adrenals kick in, providing a minor squirt of energy, just enough to lift my eyes and watch the door.

How many times have I done this? Twenty, thirty?

Here we go.

And here she comes.

Hold on ... Very attractive, wearing a flowing sundress, white moonflowers on blue cotton. Leather sandals. Nice walk. Nice feet. Nice face.

I rise, smile and extend my hand. I've become a robot.

She moves past the hand and hugs me, light and easy, then takes her seat. Relaxed and confident, with less of the southern drawl in person. Her age was given as sixty-two, but she looks younger.

The Italian waiters sense an imminent romance and swarm the table. Lighting candles, bringing warm homemade bread with olive oil and balsamic vinegar in a side dish. Smiles, winks and a wine list.

Just when I thought it couldn't happen; it has. Well, maybe.

Really?

Have I learned anything yet?

One glass in and she reaches across the table and touches my hand. A quick bolt of static electricity settles into a gentle caress.

"I'm having such a good time," she says, "thank you."

On cue, the waiter with the reckless mustache, somewhere between Cyrano de Bergerac and Wyatt Earp, glides forward and empties the rest of the bottle into our glasses.

One bottle down and dinner arrives, along with another bottle; can't remember ordering the wine but that's of no consequence, not when love is on the gentle breeze coming off the man-made lake. The Amex card is pulsating in my wallet; I'm all in. Talking about my life, my past two marriages, my disdain for online dating, my great luck in being here, now, with her. Rebel reciprocates and pretty soon, once past former spouses, online disaster dates, and mutual admiration for each other's taste in clothing and ink, she particularly likes my French leather boots while I love the small tattoo of a pink rose on her right hand, we are talking about musical tastes and favorite musicians. It feels familiar, because I've been here before, musically, with Kristan and Angelina, and Josey, and others whose names escape me but now occupy a single line space on the Elder's "list."

Seems common ground is what we all look for, and music is an easy common ground, particularly when Rebel says she's still a big fan of the '60s acid rockers, Steppenwolf.

More common ground, because my old band once toured with Steppenwolf; it was in the 1980s and not exactly at the peak of their career, but we shared a stage for four or five gigs, and although I may have said hello to Steppenwolf founder, John Kay, once, it makes for good dinner table fodder, particularly after the second bottle of wine.

Rebel suggests we adjourn to her car and listen to "Magic Carpet Ride" on her surround-sound system. Couldn't think of anything I'd rather do.

A subtle hand signal to Wyatt Earp, an exchange of confident alpha male glances as if to say, "mission accomplished and thanks for the support," pay the bill, tip magnanimously, stand up, wait for knees to adjust to a new position, take a gentle grip on Rebel's arm and head for the parking lot. If this were a sitcom, I'd expect applause from the waiters.

Then ... Cue the canned laughter.

There are two cars parked at the end of the big lot, with two empty spaces between them. Both are black, and both are spit-shined clean. A brand-new Tesla Model S and my four-year-old two -door Infiniti Q60.

Rebel guides me towards the Tesla. Opens it up. We climb in. Actually, my first time inside one, and I'm amazed at how spacious it feels; the onboard computer that looks like a movie screen. She presses a few buttons and the entire interior lights up with a warm glow. Feels like I've boarded a UFO. Another press and there's music, throbbing through the wrap-around speakers. A couple more buttons and it's 1969 and John Kay's swaggering voice is taking me away.

Well, you don't know what
We can find

Back to the Brandywine Club, on the outskirts of Philadelphia, when my band first took the stage in front of a crowd of outlaw bikers, all waiting to see Steppenwolf perform "Born To Be Wild." Not wanting to be booed off or assassinated mid-song by a flying Bowie knife, we launched into an original rocker, titled "American Hero," got a round of applause and retained our lives.

"American Hero," I wonder?

Steppenwolf winds down and I ask, "Do you have Spotify?"

"I'm on it now," she answers.

"See if you can get a song called 'American Hero.'"

"Who does it?"

"An old band; they were called Revenge."

Sure enough, after a little searching, it comes up, and the Tesla is alive and throbbing with the sound of heavy rock, and another swaggering voice from another era, another life, a voice I haven't heard in years.

"Classic eighties," she says.

"I'm not sure what that means, but her body is moving just enough to let me know that, at least, I'm not getting knifed or booed off the stage.

"That's me," I answer.

She does a double take. "What, that's you … singing?"

"Yes, with my old band."

Rebel leans across the seat and plants a sizeable kiss, smack on my lips.

A few more bodily gyrations, another kiss and "American Hero" trails out, with a heroic guitar solo, a drum roll and a Rebel yell.

There's silence in the UFO.

Then …

"Would you come visit me at my house? It's right on the lake; I'd love you to see it," she says, a little more drawl, and a little more whisper.

I feel like a balloon. My ego inflated with helium and soaring towards the 1980s, when the body was pain-free, and the mind knew no limits.

"Sure. When?"

She promises a text in the morning, arranging a time and a date for the lake house rendezvous.

Forty years peel away like skin from a snake. I'm a rocker, again. Anything's possible. *"Born to be wild. I never wanna' die.'*

"Where's your car?" she asks.

I point to the Infiniti.

"That's cute."

Cute? Sounds like something Josey might say, when admiring a new match's sexual organ.

"Is it a Fiat?" she asks.

"No, it's an Aston Martin," I say, already out the door. "See you at the lake house."

Am I learning anything?

Am I listening to myself?

Drive home singing old rock songs and trying to keep my speed below a hundred. Aside from the wine, I'm on a natural high. Higher than I've been since … Sarah …. Michelle … Kristan … Angelina … Josey …. The list goes on.

Learning anything, yet?"

Come on …

*

Morning comes. The sun is shining. The leaves are dancing in the light breeze.

"Hope springs eternal."

Ping.

Look down at the phone; it's from Rebel, my new love. No doubt to set up our next date, at the lake house.

I open the text.

And … Here comes that Bowie knife, headed straight for my heart.

You mentioned during our dinner conversation that you left your first wife and married a younger woman. To me, this shows you are a man with no integrity, no moral fiber and display a total lack of character. People don't change. I've had this happen and it hurt. I cannot be involved with a man like you. Plus, I've googled you and you are older than you said you were. So, you are also a liar. I never want to see you again.

I feel gutted, as the curtain falls, and the stage hook appears, grabbing the old rocker by the flat seat of his ancient leather pants. Dragging him away, *On a magic carpet ride …*

***

~20~

In the infinitely wise words of the Elder.
"Why do you keep doing this to yourself?"
Yes, I get it. Finally, irrevocably.
Why don't I just stop?
Let go.

I've had a great life, a charmed life. Had my marriages, my children, my houses, my career, my triumphs, my defeats, my loves and my losses. Perhaps it's time to retire. Find a gated community where I can play my guitar on the front porch, shout obscenities at passersby, and wander the sidewalks with a glass of wine in my hand, wearing only a pair of high black socks, courtesy of Outlaw George.

Accept.
Surrender.
Fuck it.

And then, one hot and sunny morning in August, many mornings after the loss of the button fronted Calvin Kleins and many more mornings after the spitting rear wheels of Josey's Hummer, and many, many mornings after the snow-white rafter and the hanging man, I stumble down the stairs, drop a tab of blood thinner, and sit down at my computer.

I rarely go on the dating sites these days. In fact, I've resigned my membership to the big one, and given up on another site that was designated for people with a spiritual intent, although strangely, many of the same faces appear on both. Does this indicate a dawning spirituality amongst the billowing supply of senior singles, or more likely, a real desperation to find a match, anywhere, with many choosing to go the holy route.

I bow to the divine in you.

Namaste.

One site, however, remains, and on this site, it is the woman who is required to make the first move, send the first photo, and write the first message. And, on this site, I have given my actual age. Thus far, I've only had a couple of messages and did not respond. Playing hard to get? No, not really. It's more like experience mixed with intuition that tells me that a match with any of them is unlikely. Maybe it's just a hunch, a feeling, something in their smile, or their eyes, or their written profile, or perhaps it's in the answer to one of the required questions, including who my potential match would most like to have a one-on-one dinner with. No offense, but Engelbert Humperdinck is not my first choice, and he probably does not want to have dinner with me, either. I cannot really say what would actually warrant a response, particularly since I am fairly burnt out in the online department. Despite this, there's a new notification in my mailbox. "You've created quite a buzz and Isabelle has sent you a message."

Isabelle? Haven't heard that name in a while. I believe it's French; sounds exotic. In fact, I don't believe I've ever actually known an Isabelle.

I go immediately to the site and read her message.

"Hello. Hello."

The two words look rather small and anemic in the large message box. Certainly not too stimulating intellectually and there's no hint of a wild sexual adventure but ... Stop ... Look at the face, the eyes, the smile, back to the green eyes. The vibration coming off the screen. Yes, the vibration.

"I know you," I say to the redhead. "Isabelle, I know you."

More pictures: Isabelle in a party dress. Isabelle dancing. Isabelle smiling a different kind of smile, sort of naughty smile. One line in her profile grabs my attention. "Dress up, dress down, or don't dress at all." It goes with the mischievous smile and makes me laugh.

"I know you." I say it again.

Scroll down.

Who does she want to have dinner with? Engelbert? Fred Astaire? Marilyn Monroe? Brad Pitt?

Actually, it's Jane Goodall, an English anthropologist who left her royal life as a titled baroness and moved to Tanzania, devoting sixty years to preserving wildlife. Jane Goodall, the world's foremost expert on chimpanzees.

Not the typical response. Chimpanzees? A social order in which the female has been known to cannibalize the dead body of an alpha male, dining out on his sexual organs. Better be on my guard.

Still, "I know you."

"I know you."

I've never quite had this reaction to an online face, or an online message, particularly one that says nothing except, "hello, hello." This is new, something that triggers some primordial recognition deep inside me. I search my memory. Can't place her. High school? The senior prom? A college classroom? Another life? The site says she's originally from Chicago and now lives in Venice, which, at eighty miles away, is just a hop, skip and jump down the road. Actually, more like an hour and a half, or maybe two and a half, depending on traffic.

The online conversation begins.

'Hello, hello, Isabelle, what do you do in Venice?'

Hours later.

"I'm a painter."

An artist. Yes, she looks like an artist. The way she dresses, like a Spanish dancer, or maybe it's not the dress but the slant position of her body in one of the photos, where she appears to be moving, dancing.

"What kind of painting?"

She sends a link to her website. Looks like acrylics, modern, swirls of color, cascades of light upon the canvas. Beautiful. Mysterious. Lists of galleries, celebrities who own her work. My brother is a painter, and he's very good. I send him the site, ask what he thinks. He emails back, who is she; the work is brilliant?

"Want to talk on the phone?" she asks.

"Of course."

We set a time and I give my number, which seems to be online etiquette. Men first, I suppose to avoid unwanted harassment.

The phone call is also easy, like two old friends, we talk about travels, painting, how it compares to writing as a solitary pursuit. She's been married, but not for over thirty years, so has spent long amounts of time alone, a thing that I'm still adjusting to. Listen to her voice, low and smooth. Experience the same feeling that I had when I first saw her face; I already know this person. I've already heard these words. Maybe I should return to the spiritual singles site; feels like déjà vu. We agree to meet, and she says she will drive up on the weekend for morning coffee, if I pick a spot. That's a change. No candlelit dinner, no vacuumed Infiniti in search of a Tesla, no deep glasses of Pinot Noir in search of a place where everything looks just a little better than it really is. No helium inflated ego and fat kisses; lips throbbing to yesterday's voices and forgotten songs. This is here and now, and everything seems different.

Because it is, or because I want it to be?

Or, just maybe, because, at last, I'm waking up. Beginning to feel at home in my own skin, and ready to allow someone to show me theirs, to share their story, without the façade that is so often projected before anything gets real, and the shadows crawl from the basement.

Her text follows.

Please don't plan something special. My wish would be to sit outside, beneath a tree and talk, get to know each other. Tell stories of how we got here, to this place in our lives.

I'm willing. In fact, I really want to.

Text back. Suggest an outdoor restaurant at the other end of town. A cup of coffee before we adjourn to share Satsang beneath the leafy branches.

Yes, Sunday morning at ten.

Consult the Elder, "Why not?"

Consult Elaine. "She's coming."

*

Sitting there at quarter past, looking at the small parking lot in front of the restaurant, waiting for her car, wondering what it will feel like to see her, to meet her, what our first interaction will be like; I feel a gentle touch against my hair, someone behind me.

"Hello Richard."

I turn, smile. No jump to my feet, no handshake, no robot. Check her out. Shorter than I'm used to, maybe five feet four. Definitely not the long-legged gum chewing sinewy type that inhabits the local gym, holding less interest for me than a set of dumbbells. No, there is something artsy here, bohemian, like a painting by Matisse, with full breasts and an hourglass shape.

"Isabelle?"

She smiles back, that same smile from the photograph, naughty but nice; sits down across from me. Dressed simply, in blue silk, the fabric long and wrapped round her body. She's older than her photograph, but so am I. Doesn't matter, not at all, because this interaction feels different; it's Isabelle's essence that attracts me, her aura feels subtle, but palpable. I feel her presence. No hiding. Just being.

"Where did you park?" I ask.

"In the lot across the street. I got a little lost, that's why I'm late. Sorry."

"It's all right. What may I get you? Breakfast? Coffee?"

"Just coffee. I love my coffee."

I'm up, feeling her eyes on me, figuring she's checking me out, too, making me self-conscious about my bowed legs and cowboy swagger. Then there's the flat ass.

Inside, and back out with a cup, nervous, but nervous in a different way. Nervous because there is an energy between us, some kind of immediate chemistry.

She sips, I talk, about the little town I live in, about my sons, about my breathing exercises, my meditation, my stalled career as a writer of books. My time alone. I always have trouble with that one, but it feels okay to talk about it, with her. She's not passing judgment. Neither am I.

Then, I listen. She has a mother in Chicago, two sisters, no children, no pets; she's used to being alone. Sometimes nomadic, and every year spends two months in Barcelona, painting, seeing friends, creating jewelry. In fact, she's scheduled to leave in two weeks.

My heart sinks. I've just met this lady and already she's gone. But why should I care? I don't know her. I don't love her, at least I shouldn't, not after fifteen minutes and a cup of coffee, but already I'm bemoaning her departure. Things become suddenly, to me, more urgent.

"Isabelle, I know you want to sit under a big tree and talk about our lives, but that means a public park and people around. I've got a big tree back at my house. We could go there."

I wait.

Isabelle hesitates.

I can feel her thinking. Does she trust me? Should she? Prepared to go off into the woods with a desperado who walks like he's spent too many years riding the range, out mending fences?

I hope I haven't pushed it. Gone too fast, too soon.

Finally, she answers, "I'll follow you in my car." I get it. At least she'll have an escape vehicle if things are less than comfortable.

I idle in front of the lot till Isabelle's blue Toyota SUV appears. Then, off we go, down the long avenue with the orange groves on either side and the mountain ridges beyond, floating like ghost ships in the early mist, headed for the ever-changing driveway. Into the mystic.

Forego the big oak tree and sit, facing each other, on the sofas in my living room. Talking. I'm midway through my reasons for leaving New York and moving out here when she raises her hand. I stop.

"Sorry, but I forgot something," she says. Then, standing, she walks towards the front door.

I have a moment. Is this it? She's leaving? Why?

"Something for you," she says, opening the door and walking towards her car.

When Isabelle returns, she's carrying a small painting, which she hands it to me.

"Hope you like it."

I take the canvas, moved by her gesture. It's an abstract, and peering through the swirls of greens, I see a tree, delicate leaves stretching and merging with a blue-green sky.

"Thank you," I say. "It's beautiful." Find a place on the shelf; the painting looks like it belongs there, in my home.

Isabelle looks at me again; pools of light inside her eyes, drawing me inwards.

Here it comes, that calm, quiet voice, entering me. "What is it you want most out of this life?"

The words fall from my mouth. "Self-realization. I want to stop living in fear. Be everything I can be." In any other context, my words would have, to me, sounded banal and sentimental, but right here, right now, I mean them.

Pick up my guitar. Hello, Engelbert ... Play a little bit. It's easy to play when someone is listening. Truly listening. Music becomes a revelation of the heart, both hearts.

"I want to kiss you," she says.

I put the guitar down and glide between sofas.

Put my arms around her.

The kiss, light and soft, with an intimacy that I've not experienced in a very long time. It's not a sexual kiss, no gouging tongues, no groping hands; it's light, exploring, and kind. Feels like two souls who have met again upon this journey, more towards the end than the beginning, both a little worn, a little tired. Taking respite in each other's arms.

Then, I push it one more time.

"Want to go upstairs?"

Another hesitation. Maybe a glance out the door at the midnight blue escape hatch.

Is she about to bolt?

"Yes, but I'm not going to have sex with you," she answers.

"Dress up, dress down, or don't dress at all," I say, repeating my favorite lines from her profile.

She laughs.

"Come on," I say.

I lead the way. Up the stairs. Into the bedroom. Past home to much internal drama. Isabelle stands beneath the snow-white rafter and within the call of the wise old owl.

"Or no clothes at all," she says.

And, with that, she slowly undresses in front of me, with the sun streaking through the wooden blinds, painting her body in shadowed shades of gold. Naked. Vulnerable, but at ease. She smiles that gypsy smile.

I'm lost for words.

Well, not quite.

"You've got the best tits I've ever seen."

*

We kissed. We touched. We held each other, but we did not make love on that hot afternoon in August. We did something else; we struck the spark for things to come.

***

~21~

Days pass, I receive an envelope in the mail; it has Isabelle's Venice address on it. Open it. Find a card; a hand-done drawing of a mermaid, in blue.

Inside, it reads, "I have a crush on you, and it feels splendid."

A crush?

I haven't heard that word in years; a crush is something I associate with school children and giddy laughter, but there it is, she has a "crush" on me.

How do I feel?

Flattered. And a little uncertain, also a bit frightened of investing my emotions in someone who travels, is very independent, has been on her own for over thirty years and seems so quick to express her feelings.

Am I setting myself up for a beating?

Remembering the words of the Elder, "Why do you keep doing this to yourself?"

But ... a crush is still light, and playful. I can handle Isabelle's crush. I think.

I text and thank her for the card, then suggest we meet once more before she's gone. It's my turn to drive, so I propose a trip to Venice, and a sleepover at her place. I have a compulsive desire to make love with her before she departs.

Watch out, I tell myself.

You can handle it; another voice reassures.

Maybe this is the way it feels, when you first set foot in quicksand and the ground that you thought was solid begins to give way beneath you.

Nervous.

Stay calm.

A trip to Elaine's, not to draw a card but to purchase a small piece of jewelry, a pendent with the word "'Love" hammered into the soft silver. Something Isabelle can take on her travels. A reminder.

I can handle it.

Two months? What's that in the scheme of things?

I don't even know her, not really, not yet. Who knows what can happen in two months?

I'm free.

Receive her reply: *That would be wonderful, please come for the night.*

*

She's wearing a low-cut purple dress, tight around her body with visible cleavage and bare feet. She's actually dressed up, not down, for the evening, even though we've agreed to stay at home, in her apartment, which is comfortable, minimal and decorated with her artwork, photographs and artifacts from her travels.

The downstairs is one big, open room, with a long beige sofa, a wooden dining table and a small adjoining kitchen.

We sit on the sofa.

It feels different in her domain; I'm less sure of myself, minding my manners.

Two strangers. Chatting. Laughing. Still getting to know each other, yet there is an attraction, some underlying sensuality, a knowing of what is to come.

"A glass of wine?" she asks.

"I'd love one," I answer. Maybe two, three, or how about an entire bottle. Watch as she gets up from the sofa and walks towards the kitchen. No, Isabelle is not tall and willowy, but she is shaped well, shoulders tapering down to her waist, full hips; womanly, but in a room full of people I would not single her out, not by looks alone. Probably just walk on by, but if we spoke, that would change things. It's who she is, and the way she thinks that attracts me. The directness, the inner strength, the insight and sensitivity that makes her an artist. Independent. Much more alluring than long legs or a pretty face. And, maybe, more dangerous. If a relationship is based upon need, and I know I've got some, these are the qualities that could also sink it; there's no co-dependence here. I caution myself, be careful, then remember Elaine's cards. "The Queen of Wands. Your equal. She's been waiting for you."

Waiting?

Really?

Another glass of wine; I remove the "Love" pendent from my pocket and hand it to her, like a schoolkid might hand his "crush" a valentine; she smiles, seems touched, holds it gently in her palm, then places it on the table and picks up the vapor pipe, taking a long draw from the clear glass stem before offering it to me.

I'm feeling so vulnerable, like a child, bearing gifts, wearing my heart on my sleeve. I am not in love, but I want to be. I am not healed, but I need to be.

She offers me the pipe.

One inhalation, two, another sip of wine, relaxing. Let me have that pipe again, just once more. Love the way her skin caresses mine when she passes it to me. Settle back against the sofa. I'm safe with her, here, in this place. At peace. Bend over, kiss her gently on the lips. Can't take my eyes off those breasts, large and full, perfectly rounded; I remember her pink sensitive nipples, her warmth, the touch of her body against mine, with the sun streaming through my bedroom window.

"Want to go upstairs?" she whispers, her voice as seductive as the vapor.

"Yes, I do."

Up the carpeted stairway to a candlelit bedroom; the hint of sandalwood incense in the air, and headlights from the street below, flickering like fireflies through the curtains. People's voices, far away. We're in a different world. Tapestries hung on the walls, a wood carving of the Buddha, books by the bed.

Soft linen sheets. Sultry jazz playing from a radio. Warm kisses. Touching. Caressing. I love the smell of her skin. Her hands are exquisite. Artist's hands. Healing hands. No holding back. No restraints. Clothes come off. Feels so natural, like I've known Isabelle forever. Sex, pure uninhibited sex, but it's more; it's a connection, deep and primal, a man and a woman, making love. Talking. Laughing. At ease with each other. Time dissolves as minutes become hours, blending with the rhythms of the base guitar, the drums, a smoky saxophone, as our two bodies become one body, and then ... oh no ... one part of my body is no longer participating in the dance. Self-consciousness swoops like a bird of doom; I wonder if she notices. Doesn't seem to, so I continue to move but it's impossible to stay inside her when the physical gives way to the mind; and the voices begin. "What will she think of me? This never happens. But it has. Why? Why now, with her? What do I say?"

Slowing to a soft halt.

Whispering, "Isabelle, I'm having a little trouble." Her eyes look into mine. She smiles.

"But I've got a pill." Then, handing the decision to her, as if it's her problem, not mine, I add, "Should I take it?"

She never stops moving, using her body, her hands, anything to reassure the noble tiger.

Answering, "No." Rubbing downwards, a little closer to my shyness. Wrapping her warm hand around me. "Maybe later, if you want, but, for now, it's not important."

Slow inhalation, long exhalation, pause. Her hand feels good, friendly and familiar, like my own, but kinder. I trust this woman.

A few seconds pass.

Low and behold, there's life.

Our lovemaking continues, tender, explosive and honest, till the first rays of sunlight snake through the white curtains. And now, the gentle peace, the aftermath, lying together, quiet, my arm around her, her head resting on my chest, and that wonderful silence between thoughts.

"I love you."

No, that wasn't me, not my voice.

"What, what did you just say?" I ask, like perhaps Isabelle is talking in her sleep.

"I love you," she repeats.

"Why?"

"My heart is open."

"I love you, too," I answer, but my heart still has shudders, half-closed against the pending storm. "Let's go have breakfast."

Dressed. Walking the avenue. Feels strange to have a woman beside me. People pass, mostly younger, joggers in sweats, women with small dogs. My knee hurts. I tell her. I want to be Superman, unbreakable, and it feels like a confession of vulnerability.

"Then let's go in here," she suggests, guiding me by the arm to a nearby café.

We sit down inside. Order.

Oatmeal for me, something called a breakfast bowl for her. And coffee. Sipping it as I scan the other tables. Couples. Singles. Laughing. Talking. And, here I am, with a partner, not a projection, a real-life flesh and blood human who I respect; it seems so simple, and maybe it is, once the façade has given way and the heart finds its path. Two ordinary people, having oatmeal, and ...

"What the hell is that?" I ask, peering into her white porcelain bowl. Looks like rice and beans and some kind of greenery, with a couple of fried eggs on top. "You can't eat that."

Isabelle looks up, over the steaming food; her green eyes turn hazel, a flash of fire.

"I'm from Chicago, I can eat whatever I want to eat."

My equal.

"Sorry." Digging into my boring oatmeal with raisins and wondering what the breakfast bowl actually tastes like. Doesn't look bad.

Finally, it's time to pay; I reach inside my pocket. Nothing. Empty.

"I must have left my wallet somewhere," I say.

She looks at me, half a smile playing on her lips.

"I'm serious," I add. "I think it's in my car." Then, saving face. "You stay here, I'll go get it."

Isabelle shakes her head and laughs. "Don't worry, I can handle this one." Picks up her purse, digs in and comes up with a few bills.

I like this woman; I really do.

My equal.

Two days later and Isabelle is gone, to Barcelona, six thousand miles away.

And my heart, my silver heart, travels with her.

∗∗∗

~22~

It is said that we are each other's teachers. Some lessons are short, others long, some sweet, others harsh, but no one person comes to another without something to teach, and something to learn.

I'm scared of this woman. She frightens me because she's honest; there's no hiding from her, because she is a woman, not a little girl masquerading, not an ego in drag.

Am I equal to this?

This woman.

This lesson.

*

Photos flood my text: Isabelle at the airport. Wearing the silver heart on a chain round her neck. Isabelle boarding the flight. Isabelle waiting in London for her connecting flight. Isabelle in Barcelona, at her first hotel, with a big overhead fan and mosquito netting around her four-poster bed.

Wish you were here.

I love this. Almost like she never left.

It's been four days since I've seen her.

From Isabelle: *I am going to miss you. I woke up fearing my season of leisure is now behind me ... winter brings my work for the galleries, and more sales, I hope, a new collection ... then maybe a move to a new studio. I hope we can weather it and be supportive with one another ... it is my intention to do so. Please let's both do our best to remember patience ... & faith ... I love you.*

From me: *Going to do my best. Must work hard to establish my new business with the breathwork. To begin a new book. Yes. Supportive. I'd like to be kissing you right now. I love you too.*

The texts continue for two weeks; they are informative, loving and romantic, then, one morning I get the ping! and open my phone to find a black and white photo of a naked woman. Very erotic. The shot ends at the neck so there's no telling exactly who it is, although I've got a good idea that it's not a body double.

Text back, *Isabelle, is that you?*

Yep.

Text back: *Beautiful, please send more.*

And she does, a bit more graphic.

Your turn, she pings.

Wait a second ... My turn? Naked pictures at seventy-three? Now, we *are* talking about a body double. Still, I'm certain with the right light, and the right angle in the mirror, I could come up with something presentable.

Thinking about where to shoot my masterpiece, when ...

Ping!

Another shot of Isabelle, taken from an angle that suggests an extreme yoga posture with the camera looking up from the floor, in living color. I contemplate the view.

My turn?

The stakes are getting higher.

This is the art of Senior Sexting. Am I up to it?

And suddenly, out of nowhere, I feel threatened. What kind of woman sends naked photos from a hotel room in Spain? Suitable for a "mature woman's" porn site, the kind I've visited during severe bouts of writer's block. Isabelle is obviously experienced. Has she done this before? With who? How many?

Jealous?

Yes.

I'm also excited.

And she's not letting up.

Ping! *Waiting for yours.*

Obviously, an "I'll show you mine if show me yours," situation. And she's just shown me hers, so I've got to show mine.

Should I strip naked and head to the gym? That's where the full-length mirror is, last used with Josey, and responsible for a very unflattering view of my ass.

Ping!

Well?

Never done naked texting before and I feel out of my depth and under pressure.

Ping!

Back at her.

Be patient. Need to get my clothes off.

Forget the gym. It's too Neanderthal. Don't want the suggestion of Olympic bars and gymnastic rings in the background to destroy the atmosphere. This will require a certain level of sophistication. Head into the bathroom on the ground level of my house. Adjust the lights, till I find the most flattering glow. Take off my T-shirt . Flex my pecs. Hit the ground, do a few push-ups, pump it up. Not bad. Ruffle my hair with my hands. Going for that casual, who gives a fuck look, a naked man, natural, at one with his skin. Drop my pants and pull down the Calvin Kleins in one fluid motion. Face myself. Jesus. Looks like I just came out of an ice bath. Can't send that. A little self-stimulation. That's better, and it looks natural enough, like it's always that way. Okay. Limited time before it subsides. Lift the iPhone. Turn to the side and flex the abdomen just enough to hide any excess in the stomach area. Snap! Snap again, different angle. Must remember to delete these before anyone finds them by accident. Let's see what I've got.

Yeah, there I am, in all my naked glory, standing right in front of the blaring white toilet, with the seat down, and a roll of paper with a few sheets streaming to the side. Very suggestive. Like maybe I've just used it. Delete. Try again, more self-stimulation, move to a different position, clear of the bowl, and using the beige shower-curtain for a backdrop. Camera up. Smile. Got it. Oh yeah. Snap again. Smile wider, like I do this all the time, cocksure. Snap. Snap. Snap.

Let's take a look.

Very respectable, plus a happy shadow that accentuates the groin, adding a bit of mystery to the composition, and I don't look a day over sixty-eight.

Hello Isabelle, lucky girl, here I come.

I'm moving fast, very excited as I highlight the photo, type in the first digits of her phone number, the area code; and the rest is automatic. Hit send.

Wait for her response.

Nothing.

Five minutes pass.

Still nothing.

Come on, it isn't that bad. I look down at the phone. Go to messages, just to check it out. Admire the artwork. Wonder what she's thinking. Go to Isabelle. There's nothing there. What? Search. Ah … there I am, in all my flaming nakedness.

Same area code, different number, but who did I send it to?

Panic, as I look down and check the other texts in the box.

Oh my God, please, no … it's my oldest son's former tennis coach, a happily married, God-fearing man at a division one university. But yes, there it is, staring me in the face, flaccid and pink. Topped by the archetypal shit eating grin.

Text quickly, "Sorry, Jim, that was not meant for you. Was going to my girlfriend. I apologize. I am not gay. Truly. Hope you're well and having a winning season."

And, to this day, Jim has never replied.

*

One month gone and following a spirited volley of nudity, I realize it's lucky that I don't intend to run for public office; so easy to see how penis flashing congressman Anthony Weiner became addicted to online sexting, although in my own defense, the congressman's sexting involved underage girls, which vindicates me, unless we include those girls under seventy. Still, there's something undeniably arousing when your distant lover tells you how turned-on she is by your naked body and various parts of it, then reciprocates by flashing her own in imaginative displays of erotic contortion.

But I tell myself … it can't all be sex, there must be another side to this online relationship. Love, what about love?

My texts take on a more tempered tone.

From me: *Absence makes the heart grow fonder, and mine constantly grows fonder of you. Our connection is a bit of magic in a world that has lost most of its mystery. Call me a romantic. You and me, we may be meant to be. Does that scare you?*

From Isabelle: *Not scared in the least darlin' and I love how you linger sweetly on my mind ...... to be continued ....* ♡

And then, I don't hear from her.

A day passes.

Not a single "ping," that sound I've grown to respond to like a Pavlovian dog to the dinner bell.

Two days pass.

Three.

Desperate, I do what I have done before. Go back to the dating site, the safety net beneath the faltering trapeze artist. Find somebody new? Another face. Another projection. Instead, I find a message from Isabelle. *Hi. I'm that woman you had sex with about a month ago. Remember me? It was great. Let's meet and do it again. Maybe talk a little first, or just forget the talk and fuck some more. Then have a bite to eat and fuck again. Are you interested?*

What?

Why would Isabelle write this to me on a dating site when she's got my text?

Is Isabelle a psycho?

Who is this person that I thought I knew?

And … who am I?

Outraged. Jealous. Paranoid.

I answer, on the site. *Is this some kind of joke, because I don't think it's funny. Please explain.*

I feel extremely self-righteous.

No message in return.

The agony intensifies.

Every insecurity, every shadow, every fanged creature in my over-crowded basement charges up the stairs and crashes through my consciousness. Manifesting in pain and suffering.

Am I learning anything?

Oh … Yes.

I want to be in love. No, I need to be in love, and there's something wrong with that. The wrong is the need. How about loving myself first? Then moving on to another person.

I take a break from Barcelona. No more texts, and it hurts. Like I'm kicking an addiction. Cold turkey. I talk to friends. Get support from different factions, let other monkey minds augment my own: "You never really knew her. She's from LA, they're all nuts. Long distance relationships don't work. Get rid of her."

And then, there's Outlaw George, adding a gem of wisdom between takes on his latest TV series, "Women are like buses. Relax. Another one'll come along in five minutes."

Thank you … George …

How about taking another look at my own insecurities, issues with trust, abandonment, and self-confidence? Why didn't I address this stuff when I was younger? The answer is that most of us don't; always waiting for that next bus to come along, and it usually does, then the ride begins again, with a new traveling companion, and usually winds up in the same place. Round and round and round we go. But, at this age, I'm not so sure I want to climb on board another bus, with an assortment of overstuffed bags tied to the roof, spilling dirty laundry.

Truth is, my heart's in Barcelona, even though my mind is in pieces.

Where do I go to sit, meditate and repair?

I need a change of scene. The idea arrives with the morning light: Costa Rica; my close friend Keith owns a retreat center there, a place for indigenous medicines, ceremonies, sweat lodges and the plaintive sound of his didgeridoo rattling the moon in the big night sky. Flights are cheap. Call him. May I come? Yes. Yes. Yes … I'm booked.

In the departure lounge when Isabelle's text arrives.

Darlin' … I've been traveling for three days. Went to Galicia in northern Spain. I always make the trip while I'm here. It's green and wet and along the rocky coast. The light is perfect for painting. No WIFI so couldn't text … But you were always on my mind. Loving you. Re the message on the site. I'm sorry you were upset … I guess my humor is a bit startling for you … Yes … 'twas I thinking you'd get a laugh out of it … my mistake.

From me: *Sorry too. Didn't know what to think. Guess I over-reacted. I do that sometimes. On my way to Costa Rica to visit a friend ... Guess I don't really know you that well but I'd like to because I love you.*

Isabelle: *Costa Rica? So wonderful for you! I love you, too, but just want us to be realistic about whether we still feel this way with more time and in person ... it's been my concern that we could jump ahead of the true reality of what We are. I think my other concern may be the overwhelm of all these changes ahead for me with shows and moving studios and juggling it all with what you will be needing ... You are an 8 on the Richter scale, while I am a 4. When I am overwhelmed, I withdraw.*

*

I read her words, her gentle warning, but have no idea what they really mean. Just happy that she's back online. Feeling good, secure, and in love, because I want to be in love, as I board the flight to Costa Rica, carrying my guitar and looking forward to a change of place, of scenery and the humming drone of the didgeridoo.

Keith meets me at the other end, welcomes me with a smile that contains a hidden irony, reminding me of Dylan's lyrics, *There are many here among us who feel that life is but a joke.* If that's true, Keith is one of them, with round brown eyes that seem always on the cusp of laughter; gathering me up with strong hugs. Stuffing me into his truck then driving for hours, ending with a four thousand-foot climb up the side of a mountain. Parked on a grassy patch at the base of his retreat, which is two long buildings, each with ten furnished rooms for guests, standing like a half-crown at the bottom of another mountain. Up and up, into the cloud forest.

I arrive at the height of the rainy season, and the place is empty, with water coming down in cold gray sheets, Noah's Ark style, so activities focus on indoor dining for two, lots of catching up, online searching by Keith for a companion to share his remote getaway, and me, online veteran with several purple hearts, acting as his technical advisor.

Then, there's our daily musical jams, featuring his didgeridoo and my guitar. It's an acquired taste, the didge and the guitar, aborigine meets Woodstock, but one that has brought me great feelings of joy, elevated my consciousness and forged a relationship with a loyal and true friend.

So naturally, when Keith tells me he has fallen in love with a beauty from the Ukraine, I insist on seeing her.

Yes, Yana is beautiful. Standing in a flowered garden, displaying a Miss Universe body in a black stringed-bikini and bridging the gap between continents with the brightest smile since the invention of whitening gel.

"She wants to come and visit," Keith says as we ogle the sequence of titillating poses.

I step in gently.

"Has Yana asked you for the plane fare yet?"

"No," Keith answers.

"She probably will."

"Why would she do that; she has a good job?"

I refrain from further comment as we adjourn to the maloca, a large circular wooden structure, and sit side by side on meditation cushions for a musical interlude, with the rain pounding on the domed roof as if its sole intent is to break through and drown us.

Soon we are both on a magic carpet ride; and even after years of doing this, Keith continues to amaze me with the expression of sounds he produces from a hollowed branch of eucalyptus. Steady heartfelt drones and percussive barks, the growling of a wolf, passionate whispers and excited shouts all fill the maloca; Keith is a master.

Yet, at sixty-three, he has also experienced loneliness, feelings of growing old in isolation and that desire to find a partner, that elusive entity that I refer to as the *magical other.*

Finally, the carpet alights, and we're back to the dining room for a bowl of vegetable soup, and a ping! from Kyiv.

Keith, my darling, I want very much to come visiting with you in your beautiful palace in the mountains as soon as possible but have lost my job as an ER nurse. If you would just please wire me the money for an air flight, I will buy a ticket and be kissing and loving with you soon.

I can't hold back.

"Your new boyfriend is from Ghana."

The didge master appears mildly offended.

"Do you really think so?"

"I do."

"Let's find out," he says.

Once a champion wrestler; Keith is familiar with countering an attack, which he does as I watch from over his shoulder.

Of course, Yana, but first, send me a new photo of yourself while closing your left eye and raising your right hand.

I can't quite figure it out, then I realize his brilliance. How's a guy from Ghana going to do that, especially if he's lifted the photos from the swimsuit edition of *Sports Illustrated*?

He hits send, then turns to me.

"We'll see if 'she' is really a 'he,'" he says.

After that, I retire to my guest room, with its balcony view out over the rain-soaked mountains and valleys, with dark, moody clouds suspended like parachutes in mid-air just feet above the peaks, and a periscope's view all the way to the hazy Pacific; stand a few minutes breathing in the humidity while checking my phone for texts from Barcelona. The heart is a lonely hunter.

And that's exactly what I get, the emoji of a heart, with what looks like a little red dot beneath it. 💟 Nothing else … That seems to be Isabelle's favorite heart, sort of a signature piece, but, on its own, not enough for a man hovering twenty feet above the ground in the cloud forest of Costa Rica.

Am I learning anything?

Yes, I'm a guy who needs a lot of reassurance. *Need*, there's that word again. How do I fix it?

Sit with it. Feel it. Listen to the Elder, "Develop your emotional muscles." As Benjamin Franklin wrote in 1798, "There are no gains without pains." I adhere to this principle for most of the night.

Greeting Keith in the morning, over a cup of coffee. He looks tired, too, but his eyes are alive, with something.

"Yana called me at 3 AM," he says.

"You're kidding?"

"No,"

"You going to wire her the air fare?"

He looks at me. Smiles.

"Yana has a really deep voice and lives in Nigeria."

We both start laughing.

"The guy was in tears when he called," he continues. "I'm not joking; he was crying. Begged me not to report him to the internet service; he thought they'd arrest him for fraud, said he had a wife and four kids, was broke and never did anything like this before."

"And?"

"Sounded like a nice guy. I believe him."

"So, you *are* sending him the air fare?"

"I don't think so."

On that note we head to the maloca, a place where we are both safe from ourselves. Shaking the roof, rattling the sky, but never stopping the rain; we continue our serenade for another five days.

Isabelle phones, I'm happy. Isabelle doesn't text for a day, I'm sad.

"Will I ever hear from her again?"

"Will you ever stop asking that question?" Keith responds.

***

~23~

From Isabelle: *Awaiting first flight ... to London ... then 2-hour layover ... then flight to LA from there ... see you soon ... xo* 😜
From me: *Be safe. I love you Isabelle. Hope you sleep a bit in the air.* 💜 💥 💜
From Isabelle: *Thank you sweetheart. Can't wait to fall asleep in your arms ...*

*

Isabelle leaves the key to her apartment beneath the mat.

I enter, lock the door behind me, take off my shoes and quietly ascend the carpeted stairs. She's in bed, eyes half closed, drowsy. Strip down to my underwear and crawl in beside her naked body, inside those fine linen sheets, holding her in the spoon position. Soft and warm; feels like it is me who is coming home after a long journey.

And, knowing nothing, at that point, of the long journey ahead.

What I do know is that I love this woman, or I love the woman that I believe I know. My cup is full, running over.

My need is quenched.

Driving home, up the Pacific Coast Highway. Happy that Isabelle has returned, and already anticipating our next meeting.

There are several, at my home in front of the fire, waking up to sunshine and dancing leaves, at her place with muffins and coffee and talk and laughter. More talk and more laughter. Hours on the telephone. Sharing secrets and becoming friends, close friends. At a small restaurant in Venice, with margaritas and candlelight. Christmas with my sons and New Year's Eve in the city.

But, as John Lennon once said, "Life happens when we are busy making other plans."

Without warning, Isabelle loses three close friends in as many weeks; devastating, as she struggles to find the energy to move from her studio and into another space. Lugging rolled canvases and frames and easels and everything else she has accumulated in thirty years. One of the galleries that sells her art is closing; she must find somewhere else to display her canvases. Her mother has cancer, needs surgery. Exhausted, she feels she should return to Chicago, to be with her.

It's the perfect storm.

And the perfect lesson.

I want to help, lift some of the burden, but can't find a way in.

She's told me this about herself, "When I'm overwhelmed; I withdraw."

But I did not understand her words. Now, I get it. After thirty years on her own, Isabelle doesn't lean on anyone.

And, after thirty-six years in two marriages, I've learned to lean, but do I know how to stand?

As I rush forward; she takes cover.

I text; she doesn't answer.

I phone; she tells me that she needs to be given time, alone.

Frustrated, I tell her I am here for her, will help in any way that I can.

She thanks me and puts down the phone.

Days pass.

I am hurt, angry and … forlorn.

Then, one morning, lying on my bed, feeling confused and sorry for myself, not Isabelle, I have an epiphany. I am being selfish, in a way that I have been selfish before. Putting my need for reassurance ahead of her need to be who she is; to deal with life in her own way. If she asks for space, then I must give her space. Anything else is selfish, and anything else will drive her further away. But ... I am still afraid of losing her; based upon the fear of being on my own, standing on my own. Being self-reliant.

Alive in my own light.

Take a step back.

Another look at myself, yes, there he is; frightened, judgmental, tough, self-critical, soft. Not perfect. Never enough. Okay, I'll keep trying to improve ... till it kills me.

And now, I have chosen a woman, out of all the women in my life, who has lived in another world, with a network of friends, traveling often, with lovers when she needs them, with freedom and independence. Will she be the catalyst for my final lesson?

And why did she choose me?

Why did we both choose each other?

Remember her text: *Please let's both do our best to remember patience ... & faith ... I love you.*

Patience, and faith.

And, in that moment, I let go of the notion that the *magical other* is out there, somewhere. Realizing that I am that *other*, and there's nothing *magical* about it; the only healing I need is the healing I bring to myself.

Isabelle is not going to save me.

I am.

Let go.

*

Days pass.

And then, aware of the space that I have afforded her, Isabelle phones. Thanking me for standing by her. Giving her my support.

"I miss you," she says.

We agree to meet.

I consult the Elder, "When you next sit and talk, take the 'me' out of the equation. Listen. Don't talk. She will tell you everything you need to know. Listen."

She drives to me on a cloudy afternoon that becomes a rainy night. I light a fire, we sit; I listen.

Her concern is time, with all that is going on, she will not have time to devote to our relationship.

I want to say that is not true, that I don't need that much time, just to know that she truly cares, we'll find time, but I say nothing.

Listen.

She intends to take on a full-time job at an art gallery, managing, directing, and showing the work of other artists, selling. Six days a week.

I feel it coming and my heart grows heavy.

"I'm just not going to have any time," she repeats.

"Why don't we just see how it goes?" I answer.

Isabelle spends the night, while the rain pelts my tin roof like the rat-a-tat of a snare drum and the owl hoots from a sheltered perch. Nothing has altered between us, the passion or the caring; she leaves at 6 AM for a meeting with her new employers.

The phone call comes the following day.

"I can't do it," she says.

"What?" I ask.

"Give you what you need," she answers.

"How do you know what I need?"

"I'm exhausted; I've got nothing left. I'm sorry."

My stomach is churning. I recognize that she is overwhelmed and understand her patterns.

"You don't know what's around the corner," I say. "Neither do I. Please, think it over."

"I have," she answers flatly.

I feel something building inside me, something that's always been there, coiled and waiting.

"I'll call you in the morning," I say.

Toss and toss all night. Wrestling with demons, old and new. If this is real, this connection between us, something that doesn't turn up every day, with every online face and online message, if, after all this searching, we've unearthed the needle in the haystack, then we should at least respect what we have found. I'm not quitting.

Morning comes. I phone.

"I love you," I say, and I'm pretty sure I'm talking to Isabelle this time, with all of her cracks and flaws, and not the skewed projection of my missing pieces.

"I love you, too," she answers.

"You mean that?"

"Yes, I do."

"Then, let's meet, and whatever we decide, at least it's in person," I say.

She hesitates. Thinking.

Finally, she answers, "This weekend?"

"I'll drive to you," I say.

*

And then that thing that John Lennon spoke of, that thing that happens when we are all busy making other plans, that thing we least expect but, perhaps always know is out there, waiting, that thing called life happens ...

*

Isabelle's job ends.

Our weekend plans end.

Doors are closed and locked.

Hands in rubber gloves and faces half-hidden beneath scarves or masks.

Life as we know it ends.

Covid-19, the virus that originated in Wuhan, China, is on our breath, on our hands, on our food, under our doors, in our beds. On our minds.

It's an infection that inflames and clogs the tiny air sacs in the lungs and finally chokes the body of oxygen as it shuts down the organs that keep us alive. It's a killer.

Lock up, lock down, or don't lock at all.

My two sons, the boys I have waved goodbye to so many times, the boys I have grieved would never live in my home again, the boys at the end of that long driveway, walking away, to forever … return.

Isabelle is sixty-seven miles away, behind a closed door, alone and self-reliant.

The universe has spoken.

"Shelter at home," is what the media calls it; self-isolate. Stay apart, at least six feet from the other person. Social distancing is the new dance. Stay in place. Emergency shopping only.

Televised images of horror and graphs of the infected and the dead. Doctors and nurses, covered head to toe in rubber Hazmat suits, with oxygen tanks strapped to their backs, wearing masks, face-shields and bug-eyed goggles, bent over the intubated, viral-ridden bodies, and these brave, alien faces are, perhaps, the last thing the dying will ever see.

I recall Outlaw George, talking about the year he spent in solitary confinement, pacing his cell, five thousand two hundred and eighty steps to the mile, trying to control the voices in his head. Well, we've got phones and emails and Zoom, and people six feet away, but we are still pacing, and the voices are still there. Talking. Babbling. Offering hope. Spreading doubts and fears. Whispering. Shouting. Reassuring. Crying. Laughing. Screaming.

And somewhere, in this microcosm that is my mind, my home, and my family, my heart, my silver heart, heads for Venice.

In McCartney's words, "And, in the end, the love you take is equal to the love you make." (actually "give" but John Lennon sang it incorrectly)

I FaceTime with Isabelle, noses collide onscreen, like reflections in a Christmas ball, no room for vanities here, contact is what I'm after.

We chat.

"I love you," I say at the end of the call.

"I love you, too."

Good enough, for now, like a booster shot. If permanence is what I'm looking for, I should understand, by now, there is no such thing. No vaccine.

It is also a time for reflection, of bearing witness to my stream of thought, my moods and feelings, exercising my emotional muscles as the Elder terms them.

It has been ten years since that night in the bedroom, with that cold, devil's kiss and my wife's vacant eyes, ten years since the diamond from Argentina was removed from her ring finger. Ten years since my shock, my anger and my absolute despair.

What have I learned about love and relationships since then, from my online university? From my diverse array of gifted teachers?

From the silicone breasts to the Alien's tongue and the corkscrew kisses, from the tequila afternoons to the late-Calvin Kleins with their buttoned front. And then there's the sexual tutorials, body positioned like the twists of a pretzel, pelvic floor in full contraction, observing my posterior in all its rampaging splendor. Dancing in bar rooms, avoiding Asian cops, and hanging from a rafter in my bedroom, with visits to the ER in between, then … the experience of unconditional love from a chihuahua.

Yes, it's been long run, taking me from retirement to theoretical old age, although my arrhythmic heart still feels young.

Grateful to be alive.

But what did each of us want? Each of my "matches," my teachers, my lovers and friends.

Ask Isabelle.

"A companion," she answers.

"And what is that?"

"Someone I can connect with, heart to heart and mind to mind. And a physical relationship, there has to be chemistry."

"Long or short term?"

"I was looking for someone who will be with me for the long term."

"That's what we all want," I answer.

Thinking, there was not one of my matches who simply wanted sex, or a dinner or a quick drink. Not when it got down to it, not really. As crazy as it got sometimes; we were all searching for that *other*. No matter what we told each other in the beginning, no matter how fast we were drinking the wine, inhaling the vapor, or steaming up the windows in the backseat of a two-door car, the match always turned into a relationship, short or long-term, and that's when the tests began. Sometimes we listened and learned, at others we didn't, but ultimately the connections were not about the euphoria and the transient feeling of being in love or having sex in front of the gym mirror; the connections were about change and growth.

Am I listening now?

Am I learning?

The Elder says, "Yes, you are. You've come the full circle."

Full circle means I am no longer a client, but always his friend.

*

Today is Isabelle's birthday.

Last night we celebrated with a Zoom session, and an online shot of tequila, or two.

This morning, I sang Happy Birthday over the phone, mostly in key, and sent a bouquet of spring flowers.

No naked photos, although I still sneak peeks at her old ones, from the Barcelona days. Hoping neither of my sons drop by my office and spot the naked Isabelle, in all her busty glory, filling my computer screen.

Like so many, in this situation, Isabelle and I don't know when we will see each other again, although I've been scheming.

Texting: *Happy Birthday Isabelle! Miss you badly. Love you madly.*

Isabelle texts back: *I adore you ... If you came for a visit, do you really think we could maintain social distancing!!! Ha! That's like bringing fabulous chocolate into the house & trying not to taste ... then ... eventually .... eating the whole box!!!!*

And ... With that, I vacuum and spit-shine the Infiniti.

"Air freshener, sir?"

"Yes, please, a touch of Lysol."

Don my black Zorro mask, slip into a pair of blue, Nitrile powder-free examination gloves, grab a bottle of hand sanitizer and a pack of Clorox disinfecting wipes, hop in the car, start up and floor it, spitting a trail of gravel all the way to Venice.

No, not really.

What I really do is get out of bed, meditate and shower, sneak downstairs before the boys wake up and have a cup of coffee as I sit down to finish this book.

Thanking my lucky stars that Isabelle is in my life.

Yes, I want to see her.

Yes, I want to eat those fabulous chocolates.
In fact, I want to eat the whole box.

*

Two weeks later.

Isabelle arrives, wearing a green silk print dress and carrying a facemask. We sit in my garden, on lawn sofas that I have spread fourteen feet apart. I want her to feel safe, and coming from Los Angeles, she feels she's already taking a chance by visiting my home with me and my two sons, where things are more relaxed than in the big city.

Still, she leaves the mask off.

No awkward moments; just the joy of being together, even at a distance. There are some tears at the frustration of our circumstances and a lot of laughter, plus a genuine feeling of love. The fact that we are not touching seems to magnify the longing for expression, like looking at the chocolates in the box, so tempting.

The closest we come to contact is a glass of cold wine and a swim in the pool. I'm in my black Speedo, the same one I wore to climb Mt. Everest, and she, in her tradition of "dress up, dress down, or don't dress at all," is naked, completely at ease in the afternoon sun, her body milky white and very real, perfect in her lack of inhibition. There is such allure in authenticity, when there is no pretense and no posturing. She challenges me to races and flip turns. We're laughing like kids, accepting of each other, and being, just being.

Free … A long way from that dimly lit bedroom and the death of my marriage. Seven years from my first stab at online dating. Walking through that pixelated hall of mirrors, with so many faces, so many profiles, so many reflections of who I was, and who I am becoming.

"Hello, hello."

Isabelle is dry and dressed. Seated across from me in that twilit place between darkness and light. I like the reflection in her green eyes. It's the best I've looked in a while, vulnerable but strong, and real, very real.

"I love you," she says.

"I love you, too," I answer. And yes, we've said it a thousand times, but the three words keep taking on more and deeper meaning, as the heart unfolds and opens.

Isabelle stays till the sky is black and the stars shine.

"I don't want to leave ... but I've got to."

"I don't want you to go, but I understand."

Driving down that long driveway and into the night, leaving me alone ... but not lonely.

Epilogue

Have I listened?

Have I learned?

It's been eight weeks, two months, since we were isolated, locked-down, trying to halt the spread of the Covid-19 virus. My sons have been with me. The little boys that were fast asleep down the hall on that cold night of my soul, over ten years ago, when this leg of my journey began. Now they are young men, old enough to ride motorcycles and buy alcohol. Old enough to seek their own paths. Follow their own hearts. The other night I asked my oldest what he wanted from life. He answered, "money." I understand. We need enough to sustain us. To keep the wolves from the door. But I had a feeling that he meant more than just *enough*. My sense is that he, fresh out of college and into the world, feels that money is the *answer;* that money makes everything else all right. And there, perhaps, is his first big lesson, expressed in that single word, with all its weight, all its power, and all its emptiness. Then, with his eyes wide open, looking at me with that invincible armor of youth, he asked. "Dad, what do you want?" I paused. Thinking about my life, my travels, my aspirations, my successes and failures, my marriages, my new relationship... all the people, the faces, all the reflections... Then I thought of myself as a child, looking up into the eyes of my mother. The journey ends where it begins. My answer was simple. "Love."

The End, or the Beginning.

*****

Richard La Plante

R ichard La Plante's writing career began in London, England, in 1988; he has since written 12 published books, eight fiction and five nonfiction.

He was married with two young sons and building a 'dream house' in Southern California, when his wife of fourteen years took off her wedding ring and declared the marriage over. Catching him blind-sided, the divorce left him physically ill and emotionally shattered.

In an attempt to mend his broken heart and find a true soul connection, he began online dating at the age of 64, but was soon lost in the cyberspace of photo-shopped faces, distant places and the reality that all repair must begin with the self. Many years, many encounters, and many sleepless nights later he produced *Lonely Heart, Will Travel* in a cathartic effort to heal his own wounds while helping others navigate the quagmire of finding love after fifty.

Richard is funny, deeply spiritual and often irreverent; all of this reflected in his fast-paced, punchy and often raw, honest style of writing.

Visit him at richardlaplante.com.

More from Richard La Plante:

BOOKS

Nonfiction

Real Strength: The Lost Art of Breathing (health and fitness)

Memoirs:
Never Again: Building the Dream House
Hog Fever
Detours: Life, Death, and Divorce on the Road to Sturgis

Fiction

Thrillers (Fogarty-Tanaka Series)
Mantis
Leopard
Steroid Blues
Mind Kill

Last Day

First Born

Fantasy Fiction
Tegné: Soul Warrior
Tegné: The Killing Blow

Audio "Ear Movie"

Hog Fever

Follow Richard's YouTube channel for videos on health and fitness, book readings, original music, and more:

https://www.youtube.com/c/RichardLaPlante

website: richardlaplante.com